LIFE AND DEATH
OF A
BRAVE MAN

ABIGALE BEECHER

WESTBOW
PRESS
A DIVISION OF THOMAS NELSON

WestBow Press books may be ordered through booksellers or by contacting:

WestBow Press
A Division of Thomas Nelson
1663 Liberty Drive
Bloomington, IN 47403
www.westbowpress.com
1-(866) 928-1240

Because of the dynamic nature of the Internet, any web addresses or links contained in this book may have changed since publication and may no longer be valid. The views expressed in this work are solely those of the author and do not necessarily reflect the views of the publisher, and the publisher hereby disclaims any responsibility for them.

Any people depicted in stock imagery provided by Thinkstock are models, and such images are being used for illustrative purposes only.

Certain stock imagery © Thinkstock.

ISBN: 978-1-4497-5093-0 (sc)
ISBN: 978-1-4497-5094-7 (hbk)
ISBN: 978-1-4497-5092-3 (e)

Library of Congress Control Number: 2012908112

Printed in the United States of America

WestBow Press rev. date: 07/06/2012

This book is dedicated to the bravest man I ever knew. He wanted and tried so hard to live. Our prayers are not always answered the way we would like for them to be, but God's will be done. "For God so loved the world, that he gave His only begotten Son, that whosoever believeth in Him should not perish, but have everlasting life". John 3:16. Rick is living and has everlasting life. I thank God daily that Rick was saved and knew our Lord. Also, dedicated to our entire family and everyone who prayed for Rick. The prayers and support will never be forgotten. Without Jesus Christ in our lives, the trials and tribulations would be unbearable. I cannot imagine a life without the Lord and what we have to look forward to . . . our everlasting life and seeing Rick again someday.

I decided to write this book in memory of Rick, who passed away over a year ago. I started this book a couple months after his death. I was depressed, full of anger and hatred. I have had doubts at times whether I was supposed to do this, but God shows us the way and lets us know if we just listen. There is a reason for everything and I believe God used Rick to do just that. We know God didn't cause all the pain and suffering, but he knew Rick was tired and couldn't go on. The devil causes pain and suffering. The devil's people can destroy a person's body, but cannot destroy God's spirit inside. That lives on forever. I will always have bad days, I know, but I have had many talks with God and I truly believe I am supposed to write this book to give others encouragement, faith, the will to live and especially healthcare workers knowledge. We don't want to believe sometimes that there are evil people in this world, but it is a fact. We have forgiven them and pray for their salvations. God watches over his flock all the time and is there even though sometimes it seems like he's forgotten all about us. He is always there at the right time when we need him. It has been over a year now and our lives will never be the same without Rick. When I get to feeling sorry for myself, start complaining about not feeling well or feel like giving up, I remember Rick and the things he went through. I know I am not the only person who is reminded that if Rick could go through all this, then I can too. I pray for strength and guidance. Rick's faith, courage and determination to live was unbelievable. It is hard to imagine anyone could go through so much and survive for so long. Rick touched so many lives and brought so many people closer to the Lord. We miss Rick dearly and will never forget him, but we know we will see him again someday. I want to continue his legacy and his love for Jesus Christ by telling his story. Enjoy this novel through a family's eyes.

Abigale awoke suddenly after a long night and all that had happened the past few years came flooding back. She had heard people say that when some people are in accidents, their life flashes before their eyes. That is what happened that morning. Abigale began to sob and didn't intend to awaken her husband Sam, but could not control the hurt and sadness. Abigale and Sam had lost their oldest son the night before. Both lie there sobbing and holding each other without speaking. No words could express how they felt. They didn't expect things to end this way.

Abigale started to reminisce all that had happened and tried to make sense of why. Remembering the family history, Abigale's family had always been pretty healthy. She had eight brothers and sisters, still living. Her mother and father always worked very hard and even though they never had much, she could never remember doing without. They always had enough players for softball games, red rover red rover, tag and endless games. They had the normal sisterly and brotherly fights, but to this day they are still very close. Abigale's mother passed away at the age of 76 from natural causes. Abigale's dad had four brothers and two sisters. One brother and one sister are still living, while two brothers and one sister passed away after a battle with cancer. Abigale had no recollection of her dad's parents as they passed away when she was very young. Abigale's dad had served in the army and had fought in the Battle of the Bulge. He died in a house fire right next door to Abigale and her family. That was a very heartbreaking time.

Sam has one brother and two sisters, all still living. One brother died as an infant. His grandmother passed away after having abdominal surgery, later discovering she had MEN 1. His grandfather died ten years later. He had dealt with throat cancer at one time in his life and had a tracheostomy. Sam's father also had since passed of natural causes. Sam's mother passed away after having abdominal surgery for ulcers. She had developed a blood clot in her lung and did not survive. Sam's mother had seven brothers and sisters, four of whom are still living. One sister passed away at a young age from what they thought at the time was spinal meningitis, but now believe to be MEN 1. Two brothers passed away with cancer and one sister died of natural causes. There are many nieces and nephews on both sides. To this date, there have been twelve family members in Sam's family diagnosed with MEN 1.

MEN 1 is a rare disease involving the endocrine system. There are three different types including MEN 1, MEN 2 and MEN 3. Each type has it's own degree of severity, supposedly being worse as the number increases. Sam's family has MEN 1. MEN 1 causes tumors, usually found in the head of the pancreas and the upper small bowel. These tumors produce the hormone gastrin and are call gastrinomas. High levels of gastrin cause too much production of stomach acid. Some can be cancerous if they are not removed. Some patients with gastrinomas have many tumors as part of the condition called MEN 1 (multiple endocrine neoplasia type 1). These patients often have tumors of the pituitary gland in the brain as well as tumors of the pancreas. The tumors can also be found in other parts of the body as well. Treatment is to remove the tumors, although they can return. Most patients have to have their parathyroids removed due to high calcium levels. This disease can be well managed if followed closely and no one, to our knowledge has ever passed away from the disease itself, only from complications.

Sam and Abigale had met at the county fair at the age of fourteen. Abigale and her sisters worked at the church food stand while Sam was at the fair for 4-H animals. They made such an impression on each other that they corresponded for a couple years, dated and married at the age of eighteen. Soon after they had married, Sam was hit by a car outside his parent's home while working on his car. Soon after Abigale gave birth to their first daughter, Ariel. Liking three days to being a year, Sam and Abigale had their first son, Rick. It was a joke for years between Ariel and Rick that they were the same age for three days. Three years later Sam and Abigale were blessed with their second son, Dale. Thinking their family was complete, Sam and Abigale were surprised and blessed with a second daughter four years later named Carie. Abigale worked the evening shift as a nursing assistant at the local hospital while Sam worked nights at a local factory. It worked out well as they didn't have to have many babysitters and it gave the kids a lot of fun memories joking about their dad's suppers of hot dogs and spaghetti. They also joke about the slick bottom shoes they had to wear from the dollar store. We had good times and bad times, as all families do. We all have to live, learn and grow. Sam and Abigale's children were all good kids and would not trade a thing. Abigale went to church as a child, but got sidetracked as a young adult. The children went to church at times on a church bus or with friends. After Carie was born, Sam and Abigale began to "grow up" and brought the Lord back into their lives. He had been with them all along. They lived in the same house for thirteen years while the children were young. They had friends who lived in Florida that wanted them to relocate there. Sam and Abigale thought they needed a change because the neighborhood they lived in was not the best place to live, so they sold their home and moved to Florida. Abigale smiled as she remembered the boys crying for an hour when they left because they missed their girlfriends at home. The grass was not greener on the other side as they expected so after a year and a half, they decided to return home. In the meantime, Ariel had since married and her husband was in the Navy. Ariel would spend time with us while her husband was out to sea and with her husband when he was ashore. Ariel had already returned to our hometown when her family decided to return home. She had found them a rental house and again Abigale smiled as she remembered the boys crying for an hour because they missed their girlfriends they had met in Florida.

Abigale went back to work at the local hospital as a nursing assistant where she had worked before. She also enrolled at the local university for the nursing program. The year she graduated as a registered nurse, Ariel and her husband blessed Sam and Abigale with their first grandson.

Rick and Dale, by that time had graduated high school and Carie was a senior in high school. Sam, Abigale, Carie and the boys moved our of their rental house and bought a house next door to Abigale's parents twenty miles away where she had grown up. They wanted to be close to Abigal's parents to help them if they needed anything. They were then their sixties. Ironically, after the house fire, everyone was so helpless.

Sam worked a a correctional officer ten minutes away while Abigale still worked at the same hospital she had worked at for years.

As time went on, Rick was never able to have children due to having Hodgkin's disease at the age of twenty four. He had had to have several potent chemotherapy treatments. Ariel had since blessed Sam and Abigale with a granddaughter. Later came more blessings with Carie having a son and a daughter and Dale giving them three precious granddaughters. What a joy they brought into their lives, just as their children have. The Lord always knows what we need when we need it. We can't forget the devil is always at work too. The family has had lots of trials and tribulations, like most families do, but nothing compared to what was in store for them all.

Rick was always a jokester, even as a kid. He was forever playing jokes on someone. Abigale couldn't count the times she had turned on the faucet and got sprayed in the face because Rick had put a penny in the faucet. The other kids, or their friends, would go to sleep and Rick would put shaving cream or powder in their hands, tickle their noses and guess what . . . shaving cream or powder all over their faces. Abigale remembered one evening returning home from work, there was a string hanging in the doorway. Her first thought was, "No Rick, I'm not falling for that one". If she pulled on it, she would get a head full of water because Rick had put a cup of water up on top of the door facing. Minutes later, the neighbor boy came to the door. Before Abigale could stop him, he looked at the string, said "What's this?" and sure enough the neighbor boy got drenched. Rick laughed and laughed. Rick had a laugh that was unforgettable. Abigale could still hear it in her mind.

As a child, Rick had to wear glasses and he didn't like them. They spent many mornings before school looking for the glasses until one morning, Abigale caught Rick hiding them behind the TV. He looked so cute in them.

Rick also loved Halloween and love to scare people, especially his sister Carie. Carie never liked the movie about Halloween and a certain person in that movie. Rick would dress up every Halloween like that person and follow Carie around through the house. He had her crying one Halloween, she was so scared. Rick told her, "I didn't mean to make you cry" and just laughed some more.

Another memorable moment was one day the phone rang and Rick answered it. He was probably ten years old at the time. He answered the phone, looked at Abigale like he was in shock and just hung up the phone. Abigale ask him what was wrong and Rick replied, "Mom, I just won 5000 pairs of shoes!" Come to find out, it was one of Abigale's sisters calling and when she called back and made herself known, they all laughed and laughed, as she was playing a joke on Rick. Abigale again smiled as she wondered if Rick was thinking to himself, "No more dollar store shoes with slick bottoms!"

Ariel and Rick were riding their bikes to the store one day when Rick, riding behind Ariel, yelled at her. She turned around to see what he wanted and ran head first into a parked car, breaking off her front tooth. It scared everyone at the time and surely not funny, but they joked about it in later years because Rick always called Ariel snaggletooth after that. Ariel was happy when she got a partial to replace that tooth.

Another favorite memory came to Abigale's mind when Rick found an old transistor radio in someone's trash pit. That was one of the favorite things Rick and his friends like to do, find treasures people had thrown out. Rick brought the radio home and ask Abigale to put batteries in it. Amazingly, the radio worked. Rick sat it on the TV and the next morning before going to school, Rick ask Abigale, "Mom, does that radio only play old time music?" So funny and so cute. Abigale could hardly hide her amusement. She just smiled and replied, "No Rick, it plays modern music also". It was obvious Rick had been giving that a lot of thought. Abigale had wished a thousand times, she had kept that old radio for Rick's memory box. Since the children had been small, Abigale and Sam had kept memory boxes for all the kids for special things with the intention of having a special gift for them all when Sam and Abigale were gone. Abigale also had written notes at different intervals throughout the years and put those in the boxes. Surprisingly how fast time goes.

One of the items in Rick's memory box was a football he received when he played at the YMCA. Rick was the running back and when his last year came, the coach gave Rick the football with all the arrowheads he had earned off his helmet. Rick ask for that football shortly before his second surgery. Abigale gave it to him, asking him not to let anything happen to it. She found the football in the tote, but the arrowheads were missing.

Rick always to the end, thought passing gas was hilarious. Even as a young child, at one point, Abigale and Rick were in the grocery store. An older gentleman bent over to pick up a gallon milk and mistakenly passed gas. Abigale literally had to drag Rick out of the store he was laughing so hard. Even during his surgeries, being so sick, when he was well enough to pass gas, he thought it was funny and couldn't understand why the nurses didn't think it was funny. They told him they were used to it, it didn't phase them anymore.

As Rick and Dale grew older, Sam and the boys would go deer hunting together. Dale tried several times to get a specific large buck a few weekends in a row. One weekend, Dale was so frustrated, he shot several times and still missed the buck. The very next weekend, Rick went and killed the same buck, had it mounted and hung it in his living room. That was always a joke between the boys.

Sam and Abigale were very blessed that their children were all so close to each other. They always enjoyed being together, which makes parents proud. Ariel and Rick ended up spraying each other with a water hose when they gathered before Rick's second surgery. Rick had also talked with the oldest grandson about the importance of school. So many memories and so thankful for them. If Rick was around, everyone was laughing. He loved to have a good time. He was so full of life and joy.

At the age of 24, Rick developed a large knot on the side of his neck. Even being a nurse, I thought maybe he had some kind of infection in a gland. When it didn't go away, Abigale encouraged him to see a Doctor. He made an appointment and a biopsy was done. Awaiting the results, while Abigale was at work, Rick started reading Abigale's medical books. He called Abigale at work one day and ask, "Mom, do you think I have cancer?" Never being able to lie, I said "Rick, it could be, but if it is we will get through this. We will not let anything happen to you". Sure enough, the biopsy came back and Rick was diagnosed with Hodgkins.

Abigale was watching a minister on TV one day and he was talking about how our children are God's children and they are only ours for a short while. Abigale prayed and told God that she knew Rick was his child. Abigale gave Rick back to the Lord, if that was his will, but she also prayed that she didn't want to loose him and that he would be cured. Rick went through several rounds of chemotherapy. The doctor's had told them that if you have to have cancer, this was the easiest to treat. After several weeks, the treatment was a success and Rick was cancer free. Soon, after five years down the road, he was still cancer free.

Rick couldn't hardly stand to be in a hospital after that and when Abigale would come home from work, he said he could smell the hospital and it made him nauseated. Prayers answered once again.

In the middle 1990's, not long after Rick was declared clear of cancer, one of Sam's uncles had been having some health problems and was being treated at a well known midwest hospital. The doctor's there had diagnosed him with MEN 1.

This rare hereditary disease explained all the stomach ulcers Sam's mother had and the problems his grandmother had dealt with.

The hospital was researching this disease. They sent a doctor and a nurse to the family reunion to test everyone who wanted to be tested. Sam and Abigale was unable to go to the reunion, but when they discovered this family had MEN 1 and it was hereditary, they decided to schedule appointments for the five members of their family. The testing for this disease is very extensive. At that time, it required 15 tubes of blood to be drawn along with MRI's of the head and abdomen. Sam was diagnosed positive with MEN 1 along with Rick and Carie. Dale and Ariel were negative. The diagnosis explained several health issues the family had been having. Carie had been having blackout spells even in high school. Carie and Sam had been having faintness at times, tingling of their hands and some dizziness. Lab tests revealed all three had high calcium levels requiring their parathyroid glands to be removed and a piece of the gland placed in their arm to give them just what they needed from the gland. Sam and Carie had the surgery at a hospital an hour from their home. Rick wouldn't have the surgery. Said he was "sick of hospitals" and put his surgery off a little longer.

During this time, the endocrine specialist they had been seeing seemed uninterested in their treatment. Maybe, she was just too busy or had too many patients. Unsure of why, Sam, Abigale and their family decided to find a new specialist. They chose to go to a well known southern hospital and made an appointment for all the five members of Abigale's family. The doctor was wonderful, professor of surgery and so knowledgeable about this disease. Carie had also been diagnosed with a pituitary tumor from the old specialist, who had told her it was nothing to worry about right away. When they saw the new specialist, they were told the tumor needed to be removed immediately. Rick had also decided it was time to have his parathyroids removed there. Both Carie and Rick were scheduled for surgery on the same day. Abigale smiled as she remembered Rick and Carie joking about the two for one deal.

Surgery day came and both Rick and Carrie were admitted for surgery. Both done well, but oh how stressful for two of your children to be having surgery at the same time. Rick was up and around quicker than Carie and he went to see Carie and brought her a teddy bear. Carie still has and cherishes that teddy bear.

Sam and Rick were both also diagnosed with pituitary tumors, but with medication they would have to take the rest of their lives, they wouldn't have to undergo surgery. Sam, soon after, had to have eight tumors removed from his pancreas and abdomen at the same hospital. He also did very well and finally, everyone was home and well for the time being.

A year later, Rick was diagnosed with a pancreatic tumor. He also had the same doctor remove the tumor at the same hospital. He did well and was home once again to heal.

Dear God, Abigale prayed, give us strength.

Another year later, Carie was diagnosed with a pancreatic tumor. She was in the hospital a couple times for extensive testing, trying to get her blood sugars to drop in the 40's before they decided she really needed such a serious surgery. They decided she did need the surgery and the tumors were insulin producing tumors. She underwent the surgery by the doctor who had done Rick and Sam's surgery. She did well, but bless her heart she lost so much weight. She had to check her blood sugars for two weeks and amazingly enough, she is not diabetic now. It took her a while to get back on her feet and has done well since. The Lord answers prayers for sure. Life would be unbearable without him each step of the way.

Abigale didn't like the pattern she was seeing. Even though, this disease can be well managed if watched closely, so many surgeries can take a toll on everyone's bodies and life. Only God could have gotten this family through these stressful times. Nothing as bad, Abigale thought, as having to watch her family go through so much pain and suffering. Little did she know, it would get much worse.

At that time, counting Abigale's own family, there had been eleven diagnosed with this terrible disease.

Sam's cousin, 34 years old, had to have multiple organ transplant due to so many tumors, mainly in his liver. He spent three weeks in the hospital and doing well at this time, even though some may have returned. Nonsurgical treatments are working.

What a nightmare. Surgeries over and over. The tumors can return over and over again. Abigale kept praying for strength for them all.

After Rick was well enough after having Hodgkins and chemotherapy treatments, he was able to go back to work. He took a job in housekeeping at the local hospital where Abigale had worked for years. Rick was always a hard worker and worked at fast food restaurants as a teenager and had a paper route as a young boy. He always worked at doing something. Rick bought his first car that had a bad muffler and we could always tell when he left work because we could hear that loud car coming a mile away. While working at the hospital, Rick came home one night and told Abigale about this pretty, nice girl that worked at the hospital in the same department and he said he had his eye on her. Soon Rick and Terri were dating, fell in love and were married. Sam & Abigale and the whole family loved Terri so much and still to this day, are friends and she will always hold a special place in their hearts. Terri was so good to Rick and loved him very much. Terri was also a hard worker and worked as a manager at a local food restaurant. She worked long hours and the work was very stressful. Rick and Terri began to associate with a co-worker of Rick's and his wife. The parties began.

It was not long after that Rick and Terri were having marital problems. Rick was not coming home at night. Abigale and Sam were hearing all kinds of unpleasant stories about Rick's new acquaintances. They knew rumors run rampant, but when the same stories are heard over and over agian, some of it must be true.

Rick came to see Abigale one day and said he was getting a divorce. Sam and Abigale were devastated. Rick said he was in love with another woman and we knew it had to be the friend's wife, Lucinda. The family tried to talk to Rick, but he would go back with Terri for a while and then return to the other woman. Dale had seen Rick and Lucinda at their meeting place one day. Abigale was just sick. Rick and Terri eventually got divorced and so did Lucinda and her husband. Rick and Lucinda were married. Rick's life took a huge turn for the worse. Rick was not the same person they knew. Parties all the time and horrible stories about what happened at those parties. Sam, Abigale and the whole family were beside themselves.

Sam and Abigale's family had always been so close. If they had family get togethers, Rick and Lucinda would either not show up, be late, leave early or have something else to do. At Christmas, which was always a big deal for our family, Rick and Lucinda never had any money to spend on anyone's presents, but they never seem to have a problem finding a way to finance their parties. One year Lucinda gave Abigale some pictures from some of their parties as a gift. That was very strange. Lucinda and her daughter, Winnie, never appreciated anything they were given and acted like it was not enough. Abigale thought it strange they were so unappreciative because they really never had much before.

Abigale owned her own small business besides working as a nurse. Rick and Lucinda rented a booth at the shop to sell their wares. Abigale really enjoyed running the shop, but due to her mother's failing health, she had to close up shop after a couple years.

Rick and Lucinda visited the shop one day and Lucinda commented on how nice Abigale's hair looked. Abigale said "Thank you". Lucinda then said, "What did you do, wash it?" Rick looked at Lucinda in amazement. Not a good way to start off with your new mother in law. This sort of disrespect and behavior continued and only got worse. Abigale prayed again that the Lord would give her strength to endure.

Lucinda always seemed to be jealous of Abigale's close family and their education for some reason. Abigale was puzzled by Lucinda's attitude. Abigale knew all the hard work she had put into her becoming a nurse. Lucinda and Winnie always seemed to be looking for a free ride and something for nothing and acted like they deserved it. It was always "poor me" and "pity parties". Abigale knew Rick was a grown man, but it seemed like he was becoming brain washed. It only got worse. Abigale felt like her family was falling apart. Rick seemed to pull away from the family. If anyone said anything about not seeing him or the way he had changed, Rick would become upset. That wasn't like him at all because they had always been honest and up front with each other. It really bothered the family, but they couldn't do anything about it but pray. Little did they know, they would be needing so much more strength from the Lord as they did over the next several years.

Rick had now been married to Lucinda for a few years. He had been having some jaw spasms off and on. He had not been keeping up on his health as he should and also had gained a lot of weight. He had been to his primary doctor for tests and they could not find anything that would be causing the spasms. This went on for a couple years. One day, as Rick was eating at a fast food restaurant, he began having the spasms again, jaw pain radiating down into his chest and lasted about four hours. He thought he was having a heart attack and went to the local emergency room. All the tests came back negative. Rick followed up with his primary doctor. A CAT scan of his chest was done. They found a mass. The surgeon Rick had always went to had since moved to another state. Rick was unable to reach him and made an appointment to see a cardiac surgeon at the same hospital where he had had all his other surgeries. The surgeon was an older man, had a lot of experience and the surgery was done to remove the mass. Sam, Abigale and the family knew any surgery could be serious but also knew Rick was healthy and the mass would be removed and he would be fine again. The surgery took five hours. The surgeon came out to talk to the family and told them that Rick was on a ventilator. The tumor was attached to his heart, wrapped around both phrenic nerves that control his diaphragm. His diaphragm was not working well at the time, keeping him from breathing deep, but he would soon heal and come off the ventilator. The doctor said Rick would not be on the ventilator very long.

When the family got to see Rick, he was awake, alert, writing them notes and doing alright other than the ventilator. Rick kept writing, "Am I doing to die?" The nurses and doctor reassured him that he was not going to die and that he just had to heal.

As the round team (doctor's, nurses, professors and students) visited, the professor told the family if Rick was not off the ventilator in a day or two, they would start discussing putting in a tracheostomy (a hole in his neck for him to breathe through). This would get the tubes out of his mouth. Rick was listening to the entire conversation. (There was nothing wrong with his hearing). When the surgeon entered Rick's room, Rick wrote him a note and ask for a trach. The surgeon became upset and told him he was going to get well and a trach was not an option. The surgeon was also a very caring man. He told Rick he had been thinking about him all night, trying to decide what he should do next to help Rick get off the ventilator. At that point, the surgeon also wanted to talk to the family. Abigale and Lucinda stepped off to the side to talk to him. Rick was only six feet away, listening. He explained to Lucinda and Abigale that Rick was not able to get off the ventilator because his diaphragm was not enabling him to take deep enough breaths to breathe on his own. He said he may have to take Rick back to surgery to "tie" down his right diaphragm in order for him to breathe more deeply. After explaining in detail what the plan was, he ask if Lucinda or Abigale had any questions. Abigale said she did not and Lucinda ask, "When will he be able to go back to work?" Abigale could not count the times she had stood with her mouth open in amazement. With Rick lying six feet away, listening to the entire conversation, Abigale looked at him. Rick had a pitiful look on his face and she felt so sorry for him. The doctor glared at Lucinda and abruptly said, "we are not going to discuss that at this time". Who could even think of such a thing at a time like this? He also said that if Rick was not better by morning, he would take him back to surgery then.

Later that day, while sitting in the waiting room, Abigale overheard Winnie and Lucinda discussing taking Rick off the ventilator. They were saying, "Rick would not want to live like this. He would not want to be on a ventilator. We should take him off". Abigale was furious She interrupted and ask what they were talking about and Lucinda replied, "We were saying that Rick would not want to be on a ventilator and we should take him off". Abigale was furious and reminded Lucinda again what the doctor had said. "You are not taking him off the ventilator. The doctor told us he may have to do another surgery in the morning and Rick will be fine." How could a wife, after being told Rick would be fine even think of such a thing? They knew that if they took Rick off now, he would die because he couldn't breathe on his own. Sam, Abigale and the family were flabbergasted. Not another word was said about taking him off. Ironically, little did Abigale know that two years to that day, Rick would be gone.

The next morning, the surgeon took Rick back to surgery, tied down his right diaphragm and the surgery went well. Thank the Lord, Rick would be fine after he could heal and would begin to breathe on his own.

Rick was doing well and Ariel had to be back to work. Her work place was not very understanding about this whole thing. Sam and Abigale decided to take Ariel back the four hours home and turn around and come right back. They left late that night and arrived back at the hospital at six the next morning. They prayed the entire round trip.

When Sam and Abigale entered Rick's room, Rick was sitting up in bed. The ventilator was gone and Rick was smiling. Abigale just started crying and said, "Rick, you are off the vent!" Thank you Jesus for answered prayers. Abigale turned around to say something to Sam and he was running out of the room. Abigale was so happy, she didn't go after him. Later, she found out that Sam was so overwhelmed that he went to call the other children to tell them about Rick. They thought something was terribly wrong because he was crying. He told them that the Lord had spoke to him on their way back to the hospital and he told him something good was going to happen. It surely did. God answers prayers.

Rick did well after that and was able to return home in just a couple days.

Abigale and Sam and the other children checked on Rick often after he came home. He had been home about a week when Abigale got a phone call one evening. Rick was on the other end crying, telling Abigale, "Mom, I think Lucinda is tired of taking care of me". Abigale ask Rick why and he said, "because she told me I could get up and get what I needed and she is being real short with me". Sam and Abigale immediately drove to Rick's house the twenty miles away. When they arrived, Lucinda had friends visiting, loud music playing, laughing, talking and very surprised to see us. Sam and Abigale didn't see Rick anywhere. His bedroom door was shut and they went in. Rick was sitting on the side of the bed crying and said, "I am hurting and Lucinda will not help me or pay any attention to me". Here Rick was with a huge incision on his chest and a huge incision on his right side, unable to move well at all with no one who would help him. Being a nurse, Abigale knew how important it was for Rick to move after surgery, but he needed help. Furious again, Abigale and Sam tried to persuade Rick to come home with them. By that time Lucinda had sent her friends home and was now in the bedroom talking baby talk to Rick (one of her favorite things to do like he was a little child). Before it was over, she convinced Rick to stay there. Sam and Abigale helped him get settled, made sure he took his pain medicine, helped him in bed and left for home. Rick didn't like to take pain medication or any medicine for that matter. He was very sensitive to medicine as his mother and grandmother.

A few days later, Abigale was working and got another phone call from Rick. He was downstairs in the radiology department getting a chest x-ray. He was scared because he was having problems breathing. Abigale got off work and waited with Lucinda and Rick for the results of the chest x-ray. The technician came out to tell Rick that he had some fluid in his chest. She said, "your doctor said you can either stay the night or he would give you Lasix (water pill) and go home and see him in the morning". Rick looked at Abigale and she told him she thought it best he stay the night so they could watch him closer. He agreed. As the evening went on, Rick's breathing became more difficult. While waiting for the staff to get Rick settled, Lucinda told Ariel that Rick was a hypochondriac.

Rick's primary doctor had since left for the evening and another doctor (Sam's doctor) was on call to follow Rick. He ordered an echocardiogram (a graphic outline of the heart's movement) of Rick's heart. During this test, high frequency sound waves, called ultrasound, provides pictures of the heart's valves and chambers. This allows the technician, sonographer, to evaluate the heart's pumping action. Rick was diagnosed with Cardiac Tamponade which is a compression of the heart and occurs when blood or fluid builds up between the heart and the outer covering of the heart. This sometimes happens after heart surgery. The doctor decided to have Rick lifelined back to the hospital where he had surgery four hours away. Being a nurse on a medical-surgical unit and only worked on critical care a few times when they needed help, Abigale had never seen anyone prepared to be lifelined out in a helicopter. She was so impressed with the care they took with Rick. Very detailed and very professional. More prayers answered. If Rick had went home that night, he probably would have went into cardiac arrest. That inner feeling, God talking to us all the time, is always there if we just listen. Lucinda had left after her friend had come to give her money. Sam, Abigale, Ariel and Carrie left after the helicopter left and made the four hour trip in three hours. When they arrived, the critical care unit had Rick all settled in, had given him more Lasix and had drained four liters of fluid from around his heart. Within just a few days, Rick was home again and well on the road to recovery.

Rick's family went by often to check on him. While Ariel was visiting one day on the front porch with Lucinda and Rick, Rick went into the house for a moment. Lucinda and Ariel were having, of course, a conversation about all the events that had occurred with Rick and all that he had been through. Lucinda made the comment, "the money would have been nice but I would rather have him". Ariel was in shock at such a comment. Referring to the life insurance, that was not the only time that comment was made. That was the beginning of many instances Rick's family wondered about his well-being.

After Rick was well enough, Abigale talked to him about filling out a living will, especially after the incident at the hospital over the ventilator. Rick told us Lucinda had misunderstood his intentions. A social worker Abigale worked with helped Rick fill out a living will, making it legal. She was a real blessing to Rick's family more than once. Abigale was so relieved to have documentation of Rick's wishes. His living will stated that he wanted everything done unless he was brain dead.

After Rick was well on his way to recovery, he began to think a lot about what he had been through and the fact that God surely had a hand in his getting well. Lucinda had an aunt who attended a church forty-five minutes away and she wanted Rick to meet her minister. Abigale's brother in law is also a minister, but sometimes it is best to talk to someone who is not family. Abigale didn't mind that and was just overjoyed that Rick wanted to talk about the Lord. The minister had plans to come to Rick's home in the evening. Rick ask Sam and Abigale if they would come too. Abigale told Rick, "Rick you don't need us there, this is something you need to do on your own". Rick replied, "I want you there". Sam and Abigale went. The minister and his wife were young and very sincere. They talked with Rick for a while and the minister told Rick, "When you decide you want to ask God to come into your life, I will help you or you can go to anyone you choose". Rick replied, "I am ready now". Dear Jesus what joy! Everyone got down on their knees around the coffee table. The minister helped Rick to ask God to come into his life and forgive him of his sins. The tears flowed and flowed. Sam and Abigale thank God every day that Rick wanted this and so thankful for his decision. Now Lucinda decided she also wanted to be saved and the minister helped her ask the Lord to come into her life and forgive her of her sins. The minster told Rick and Lucinda what bible verses to start with on their new journey, suggested finding a church to attend that would help keep them on the right track. Abigale and Sam were very impressed that the minister told them it didn't have to be his church, just a good church. Rick and Lucinda decided they wanted to start attending the minster's church and they did.

Rick's minister has a disease of his own that makes it hard for him to get around. He has a lot of back pain. He still was able to get down on his knees that night and help Rick and Lucinda ask God to come into their life. Church got to be off and on for Lucinda and Rick partly because some communication problems at home. Lucinda wanted Rick to go to a party soon after he had been saved and had not been home that long from the hospital and he didn't want to go. Hard to believe, but just wait. So many things hard to believe.

As the next year went on, Rick got better and better. He did have to have some radiation treatments to his chest to make sure the doctor's had gotten all the tumor, as they did turn out to be cancerous as well as some of the others he had previously had removed. Sam and Abigale spent a lot of time with their family and thankfully, Rick was more like himself and he was included in the family get togethers. He seemed to want to spend time with them as before. They planned camping trips, even camped out in Sam and Abigale's back yard. They are all fans of Nascar and Earnhardt, Jr and would get together to watch the races every weekend they could. Joyfully, they even got to go to a race together. They always had dinners to celebrate everyone's birthdays, or just get together to eat and visit. Family time was a big deal to them all.

Abigale planned a benefit dance for Rick. They didn't make a lot of money, but over $3000. Anything would help as Rick had been out of work for a while. Rick was grateful. Lucinda said she had hoped for more. Rick wanted to buy his minister a motorized chair so it would be easier for him to get around. Before Rick could find one he could afford, the minister had bought one for himself. It was the thought that counted. Rick loved him so much.

In the meantime, during this year, Lucinda was diagnosed with diabetes. She did not have to be on insulin, only medications and with the correct diet and weight loss, could be well managed. Of course, Rick was worried about her.

In the summer of that same year, the radiation doctor had told Rick he was clear of cancer in his chest. Everyone was thrilled beyond words. Another prayer answered.

A couple months later, Rick called Abigale and Sam and said he and Lucinda were coming to talk to them. When they came, Rick told Abigale and Sam he had three tumors on his pancreas he wanted to have them removed. Rick's previous surgeon knew they were there, had evaluated them a couple years before and had said they would just watch them since they were not growing or causing any problems. Rick was worried they might turn into cancer and wanted them removed. Since Rick's surgeon had since moved and was unable to reach him, Rick decided to let another surgeon at the same hospital do the surgery. Sam and Abigale tried to talk him out of it, but Rick was determined. The surgery was scheduled. Lucinda didn't have much to say.

With the impending surgery, Rick started getting depressed, doubting his faith and not wanting to attend church. Sam and Abigale talked with Rick and told him "God speaks to us". Rick said, "I don't think God has spoken to me". Sam and Abigale reassured him that God does talk to him and he does hear his every prayer and knows all his feelings. Rick was truly saved. His life changed. He wasn't the same person he had been since he had been saved. He didn't want to party or associate with the same friends he had before even though Lucinda did. That's when you find out who your real friends are.

Rick and and Dale began to spend more time together. Makes a mother proud for her children to love one another. Lucinda didn't like that either.

Sam and Abigale had an uneasy feeling about the surgery Rick was getting ready to have done. Not like the rest, it seemed. Pretty serious surgery. Abigale printed off information about the kind of surgery (whipple procedure) Rick was going to have and gave it to him. She wanted him to know about what he had in store. Abigale hoped Rick would change his mind, but he was so afraid of cancer, he wanted it done.

In October of that year, Rick underwent surgery for an adrenalectomy (he also had a tumor on his adrenal gland) and a whipple procedure due to the area the tumors were located.

A Whipple procedure consists of removing the distal half of the stomach, the gallbladder and it's cystic duct, the common bile duct, the head of the pancreas, duodenum, proximal jejunum and regional lymph nodes. Reconstruction consisted of attaching the pancreas to the jejunum and attaching the hepatic duct to the jejunum to allow digestive juices and bile to flow into the gastrointestinal tract, then attaching the stomach to the jejunum to allow food to pass through. Very complicated surgery.

The surgery was very long. It lasted well into the night. The nurses would tell the family a couple more hours and in a couple more hours, they would tell them it was going to be longer. After several times of this, the family finally broke down with worry and was very concerned.

During the surgery, the colon was without oxygen for about four hours and part of the colon had to be removed. Rick went to critical care and was again on a ventilator. Thank God he had made that living will. Rick also had an epidural for pain management. That can lower blood pressure. The reports Abigale obtained later stated that the surgery was a tight closure, but the nurses had told the family that the incision was left open due to swelling. That was one of the reasons they had said why they did not want to turn Rick. Rick had tubes everywhere. Of course, he was unconscious and on the ventilator, thank God. His blood pressure was very low and he was sedated, but the family was told he was doing well and improving slowly. Three days later, Rick had to have two pints of blood due to his blood count being low. They tried to wean him off the ventilator, but was unable to do so. His blood pressure was still very low and had to have more medications to increase it. This affects the blood supply and healing of the colon. Rick was started on TPN, a nutritional intravenous feeding through his veins. They were also trying to wean him off the Versid, the medication keeping him sedated. Abigale was happy about that because she had told them of Rick's sensitivity to medications.

Rick began to run a low grade temperature. Blood and urine cultures were done. Carrie had also, one evening while we were visiting, found an infected IV site under Rick's wrist restraints. Abigale tried to tell the nurse and ask if it could be changed, but finally after twelve hours, it got changed. The ventilator was still being weaned. More answered prayers. Another medication they had Rick on was called Presidex, a medication used for sedation in critical care patients on the ventilator. After looking this medication up, Abigale discovered another name for this medication was "Sedation Vacation" and should not be used more that twenty four hours. It had been used a lot longer than that and the nursing staff had the authority to adjust it as they wished. Most nurses have common sense, but there is always that one or two that liked to have their patients "out" rather than to deal with their needs it seemed. Abigale never understood how someone who is already "out" with low blood pressure needs more sedation. She understood sometimes they are treating vital signs, heart rhythms and such, but they could tell Rick was trying to wake up and couldn't. By this time, Abigale was becoming "Mother Witch" to some of the staff. After all, this was her son. Eight days after surgery, Rick was responding to the staff and family talking to him. He was still running a fever. The doctor did a bronchoscopy (scope down into the lungs for specimens and to look around to ensure nothing else was going on) and to check for infection. Rick was now on a lot of antibiotics and still on two different blood pressure medications. He was so swollen in his arms and legs.

The doctor's also did a CAT scan of his chest which showed what they said they thought was possible cancer in his spine. Lucinda dwelled on this. Abigale told her it was not a positive thing. At one point in Abigale's life, doctors had told her dad he had cancer of the spine and it turned out to be arthritis showing up. Rick's CAT scan also showed bilateral pneumonia. By the next day, Haldol yet another sedative, was added. Still critical, but improving. The staff began to talk about critical care psychosis.

Lucinda then started to dwell on the psychosis thing. Abigale would see her following the doctors around, laughing and talking and the next thing the family knew, another sedative would be added. Now Rick was getting Ativan too. How could someone have critical care psychosis when he had not even been awake enough to know where he was. Very frustrating. Abigale knew where all the requests for sedation came from as you will find out later.

Rick was awake and alert after a couple more days, but still on the ventilator, still had an IV, a catheter in his bladder, drains in his stomach, IV lines for blood draws in his groin, tube down his nose into his stomach and at times, nineteen bags of fluids hanging.

The family prayed, Dear God hear our prayers. As large as the family was, everyone was praying. Abigale was also a member of a large social network online and so many other people were also praying. God hears and answers prayers for sure.

By the eighteenth, Rick was able to come off the ventilator and his blood pressure was staying where it should be. Some of the sedation had been stopped. Rick was awake and alert and trying to talk to the staff and family. They were ecstatic. Thank you Jesus. Hopefully, on the road to recovery. The cultures that had been taken from his lungs a few days before had come back with a yeast infection. The infected IV line the staff said was not infected also came back showing yeast as the records Abigale obtained later showed.

Lucinda wanted to mess with everything. While Rick was on the ventilator, she messed with the vent tubing. She was also messing with all his IV lines, his stomach and everything she shouldn't be touching. The more Abigale ask her not to mess with everything, the more she did it. Lucinda had made the comment that she could be a nurse because she already knew all about it. "All she needed was the terminology". Oh brother, if only it was that easy.

Sam and Abigale had not even thought of leaving until Rick was off the ventilator and doing much better. Now Rick was able to tolerate sitting up in the neurochair. One morning while the staff was getting Rick settled in the chair, Sam and Abigale decided to go get a bite to eat. Upon arrival back to Rick's room, Abigale seen Lucinda standing over Rick and Rick had his mouth clamped shut, shaking his head "NO". Abigale rushed into the room and Lucinda had a white powdery substance on her finger trying to put it into Rick's mouth. Abigale ask Lucinda what it was and she replied, "he wanted a mint so I crushed up a mint". In the first place, Rick had not eaten or drank for twelve days, was not supposed to and he obviously did not want what Lucinda was trying to give him. Abigale stressed to Rick, not to take anything until the doctor's said it was alright. Abigale again wondered how many times she needed to thank Jesus for putting them in the right place at the right time. Many, many times.

After the next few days, the staff continued to wean the ventilator. Rick even got up to sit in a neurochair, a chair that can fold from a bed to a chair, but he was too sedated still to tolerate it. By the twentieth, Rick was still doing well and improving. Sitting up helped his lungs and everything. Sam and Abigale really didn't expect to be there that long. That afternoon, they decided to return home and try to return to work the next morning. They didn't know if they could concentrate, but they needed to try. Rick would need them when he got home.

On the way home that evening, Sam and Abigale tried to call Lucinda several times to check on Rick. She wouldn't answer her phone so they tried Rick's phone. Lucinda''s mother, Corella answered. She told Abigale that Lucinda let her borrow Rick's phone. When they got into their hometown, they passed Rick's truck on the street. Lucinda's brothers were driving Rick's truck and without insurance, they found out later as Lucinda had dropped the insurance on the truck when Rick went into the hospital for some reason.

Abigale was finally able to reach Lucinda that night and she was able to talk to Rick on the phone. He was mixed up, but had even walked some in the hallway. Rick kept talking about eating at Buffalo Wild Wings (his favorite place to eat) and had invited one of Abigale's brothers and sisters to go with him when they had called and talked to him. Rick was still not supposed to eat or drink. Only getting tube feedings at a slow rate, 10cc's an hour. He seemed to be improving, but the confusion worried Abigale.

Abigale and Sam didn't sleep well at all. The next morning they drug themselves out of bed, got ready and went to work. Abigale no more got into the nurse's lounge at work and she got a phone call from Lucinda. She was crying, telling Abigale they needed to come. Rick had taken a turn for the worse. Supposedly, he had vomited, aspirated into his lungs. He had went into respiratory and cardiac arrest. Dear God up in heaven, please don't let him die was Abigale's constant prayer. Carie was working the floor above Abigale, getting ready to finish up her 12 hour nightshift. Abigale called her to let her know what was happening and ask her to call the other two siblings and Sam. Abigale was numb. They all jumped into the car to head for the hospital four hours away. Praying every inch of the way, crying and so upset, they sent text messages to everyone they knew, asking for prayer. Several prayer chains were started. Abigale tried to call Lucinda many times to try to find out what was happening. Lucinda told Abigale the hospital had called her at three or four in the morning to come to the hospital. She didn't think it was anything important so she didn't go right away. She had arrived and found out what was going on with Rick at seven A.M. when she gave Abigale the phone call at work. Lucinda said the doctors said Rick aspirated, coded and they were still working with him. About two hours into the trip, Abigale got a phone call from one of the doctors. Her heart sank. She ask, "Is he still alive?" The doctor told her that Rick was critically ill and they were doing all they could do. Abigale was so afraid that when they finally got there, Rick would be gone.

When they did arrive, all of Lucinda's family was already there. How did that happen? More important things at hand. The doctor's came out to tell the family they had placed Rick on ECMO. Being a nurse for so long, Abigale had never heard of ECMO. Her hospital didn't have such a thing. ECMO stands for extracorporeal membrane oxygenation. As the name implies, it refers to the delivery of oxygen by a machine, similar to a dialysis machine. It literally means by mechanical bypass that takes place outside the body. It is very similar to a heart-lung machine that is used to continue the supply of blood and oxygen while the heart is stopped, such as during open heart surgery. ECMO therapy, however, is intended for patients whose heart and lungs cannot normally function on their own. There was an ECMO team who specilizes in operating and watching the machine and patient. It was incredible. The process begins with dispensing an anticoagulant to the patient to minimize clotting of the blood. This is necessary because the patient's blood must pass through a tube to the ECMO machine where it can be oxygenated by an artificial lung and be returned to the patient's body. The machine further stimulates human respiration by removing carbon dioxide from the blood. The patient remains placed on the machine and the dialysis machine until his or her own heart and/or lungs can resume normal functioning. In this particular hospital, the ECMO machine was kept at the children's hospital as it is normally needed for children. The patients were always taken to the machine. In this instance, it was the first time in the hospital's history that the machine was taken to the patient. Before the day was over, they told Rick's family that he would probably be on the machine for several weeks. At least he was alive and they were taking good care of him. No one ever left his side.

How did this happen? After the fact, Lucinda told Abigale they increased Rick's tube feedings from 10cc's an hour to 60cc an hour. That didn't sound right because usually if they decided to increase tube feedings, it was at a slower increase and not such a dramatic increase. No wonder he aspirated. The records Abigale obtained later also stated they had done a bedside exploration into his abdomen when Rick went on ECMO to try to find a source of infection. Rick was septic (massive infection) coming from somewhere. The records also listed all the medications Rick had prior to the incident. He had, even though he was not to have anything by mouth, Quetiapine 2 tablets. This medication can cause cardiac arrest in people not used to this kind of medication. Rick, prior to admission, had been on Lexapro due to stress and the doctors were substituting Zyprexia under the tongue. That afternoon nurse did not give it to Rick because he had been to sedated. The night shift nurse gave Quetiapine, Zyprexia twice, Lorazepam twice and Oxycodone. How in the world would he be able to help himself that sedated if he had to vomit? Only a few weeks ago, Abigale was going again over the records and found a one line insert from a doctor's dictation that said, "Had beer". Abigale was flabbergasted. As it was stated earlier, all this would make sense to you and where all the medications came from. Abigale had found in the records where Lucinda had filled them out for Rick and added that Rick drank twelve beers every weekend for ten years. Abigale believed that Lucinda used this information so she could say he was withdrawing from alcohol, therefore needed something for withdrawals. Abigale believed the entire events were planned and ended as she had wished. A few days later one of the doctors that had been in the room with Rick the night he coded told Abigale, Sam and Carrie that Rick had died for twenty minutes. That was a long time and very rare that anyone would survive after that length of time. Only by the will of God.

Rick came off the ECMO machine six days after being put on it. Such a strong person and such a will to live. Medicines had decreased to only necessities along with antibiotics. Rick also had bilateral chest tubes at that time. Tubes through the outside of his chest to the lungs due to collapsed lungs caused by a collection of fluid or air between the lung and the chest wall. Two days later, Rick got a third chest tube on the left side and the right one was removed. Later that evening, the surgeon took Rick back to surgery for an exploration surgery. Rick also went back three or four more times, every other day. As Sam and Abigle found out later, each time more bowel was removed due to necrosis (dead bowel).

Cutltures previously done, showed Rick had E-coli infection in his lungs and a staph infection in the IV central line he had. He was on four different antibiotics, but he was improving, once again, slowly. Now, back on the ventilator, after being removed from ECMO, but over another huge crisis.

Abigale tried to talk to Lucinda and the rest of the family about not touching Rick, his tubes or any of the machines he was on to try to prevent any further infection. Rick's family listened, but Lucinda wouldn't listen. She would stand over Rick with her cell phone, sit and play with her computer, mess with his ventilator, shut off the monitors and mess with his belly dressing and tubes. She would never wash her hands or use gloves until after the fact. Abigale was infuriated but none of the hospital staff would listen to Abigale for some reason. Abigale had read that the dirtiest things in the world are a cell phone, shopping cart and a purse. Two out of the three things were in this situation. Abigale could not remember how many bronchoscopies or central lines Rick had during his ordeal. He had a chest x-ray every day and numerous, numerous units of blood.

The first of the next month, Sam and Abigale were on one side of Rick's bed and the nurse was on the other side. She was so good to him, didn't oversedate him and took very good care of him. While they were all standing there, Rick started vomiting large amounts of huge blood clots. They just kept coming. Abigales first instinct was to put Rick's chin down to prevent them from going into his lungs. The nurse yelled for help, Abigale's knees almost buckled. Dear God, what now? That happened again one more time that evening. The doctor came in and done a lavage on Rick and cleaned out his stomach the best she could. It never happened again. Rick was so sensitive to all medications, even blood thinners and the tube down his nose was evidently irritating his stomach. After that was over, the female doctor that done the lavage said to Abigale, "It wasn't anything the nurses done". Lucinda was standing there quiet. I thought that was a strange thing to say, but after all the months Rick had been in the hospital, she had a feeling that Lucinda was telling the staff things about Rick's family to make them look like monsters and to divert the attention off her evil doings. The way the staff talked to Rick's family, the way they looked at them, they knew something wasn't right. Lucinda had a way of getting people to feel sorry for her. It brought her lots of money, attention and sympathy, but that's another chapter.

The next day Rick had another pneumothorax and had to have another chest tube placed. Now Rick had a yeast infection in his blood and lungs along with everything else. More prayer requests sent out daily. Continuous prayers from all over were coming in and going up.

Someone had told Lucinda about a site online where she could keep everyone updated about Rick in a journal. She started it, but didn't keep it long. She made the comment to Abigale that it made her nervous and "did you know we don't get the donations that are donated in Rick's name?" Oh my, never ceased to amaze Abigale. Lucinda had put in twelve days of updates and several of them was put in by her neighbor. Lucinda had her laptop with her and the last one she put in was was about a fundraiser the church was having for them. Abigale understood good people wanted to help others, but sometimes people also take advantage. Sam and Abigale found out that Lucinda, Rick, Winnie and Winnie's boyfriend all had a joint checking account. Wasn't that strange? Two young adults having a joint checking account with their parents? Abigale would get so aggravated because Rick would lie there with holes in his socks and Lucinda and Winnie would be sporting new clothes all the time along with pedicures and manicures. Income couldn't be too bad. Winnie would go to work with new clothes and tell people that Rick bought her the new clothes which was true. If Rick needed anything, Lucinda would call Abigale and ask her to bring him pajamas, socks, water or anything he needed. She acted like she didn't want to waste her money on him. Sam and Abigale sure didn't mind getting him what he needed. Free was Lucinda's first priority. That was the first thing her and her mother, Corella would do when Rick had to go to a new place, to see what all they could get free and they acted like they deserved it all. Free rooms, free food, wanted free parking places. A free room was where Lucinda was the night Rick coded, Abigale was told, with a "girlfriend" literally. It was very embarrassing. Abigale realized how expensive it was and her and Sam found out first hand. The hospital Rick was at was building a new ICU unit at the time and the new rooms were to have a family areas in them also. Lucinda kept talking about how she wish she could stay with Rick, but when she could, she wouldn't. It's probably just as well. When she was in the room, she was always messing with something. She even memorized the code to the nurses supply cart. Who would think of doing something like that unless you were up to no good? Four doctor's came into Rick's room one day to change his dressing. None of them knew the code to the cart. Lucinda opened it for them. Not one of them acted like they thought that was unusual. Unbelievable. That made Abigale very uneasy. That cart kept the syringes and supplies. Some of the staff was very careless and left half full vials of narcotics sitting around on their carts in the room. Abigale ask them not to do that. Abigale found a half full vial under the bed at one point. Lucinda liked to play nurse.

As time went on, it seemed like Rick was really trying to wake up, but just as he would begin to wake up, he would get a nurse who like to knock him down again with medicine. Those were the nurses Lucinda liked. She didn't like the ones with common sense or the ones who wouldn't give Rick the medications Lucinda ask for.

Abigale and her family tried to stay focused on Rick through all this. It was very hard to do. It became almost like a joke when things would happen, which seemed pretty often. They would just look at each other and say "FOCUS".

Rick had a tracheostomy put in after coming off ECMO. Now as he was trying to wake up, he was trying to mouth words to the family and staff. Very frustrating for him and the family as it was hard for them to understand what he was trying to tell them. He was so pitiful.

When Rick was first admitted into the hospital, he weighed 260 pounds. In a year he lost 80 pounds. His nutrition was very poor. He had a fistula (a hole in his bowel) on his right side they were hoping would heal, but couldn't guarantee. Anything Rick would put in his mouth would come out of that hole in his side. Still on and off the vent, the doctor's were trying to wean Rick off, but he just couldn't seem to stay off long. He had one respiratory therapist that was so good to him and helped him out tremendously. She done him more good than anyone, mentally and phyically.

Rick was a big Colt's fan. Abigale made him a Colt's hospital gown and he would wear it every Sunday for the games whether he was awake or not. Carrie had bought him a Colt's blanket. Rick was always so cold and decked out for the games. People would come to the door of his room just to see his Colt's attire and the miracle man lying there.

On Rick's birthday, he was still unconscious, but his family was all there with their homemade shirts with his picture. Their shirts said, "Happy Birthday, Rick, We miss you". They wanted everyone to know what Rick really looked like and know he was a live person.

The sedation was finally turned off and Rick began again trying to wake up. The family had made him a poster with pictures on it and over the next few days he tried to look at it, but acted like he wasn't quite sure what he was looking at. Then he looked at the pictures of his two dogs. He loved those dogs and he smiled. Those dogs were his kids he could never have.

Rick still had two infections, one in his lungs and one in his blood. He was also back on the feeding tube. The hospital put him in isolation and visitors had to wear gowns and gloves while in the room. It didn't do much good when Lucinda would still stand over Rick with a cell phone, use a lap top constantly, pull her luggage down the hall to the bathroom and back into Rick's room, then mess with his tubes and ventilator. Corella, even at one point, come rolling a battery charger into Rick's room and put it in the bathroom. No one said a word. Unbelievable!

Sam and Abigale again tried to go back to work. The bills were not getting paid and it was getting harder and harder financially, but Rick was more important. That evening after returning home, Lucinda again called saying the doctor's thought Rick had a stroke. She started in with the talk about being brain dead (as his living will stated). Dear Lord, protect Rick. Abigale's first instinct was to jump in the car and return to the hospital, but one of her sister's came to stay with her while they awaited the results of the CAT scan of Rick's head. Finally, late that night, some good news. No stroke. It turned out, an optometrist had come to check Rick's eye's that morning, dilated them and didn't document it.

The middle of November, the doctor's told Rick's family that he had leaks and tears in his bowels from so many blood pressure medications. Very, very poor nutrition, which has made his bowels paper thin. Dear God, Abigale remembered praying. Maybe more surgery in a couple weeks if Rick's nutrition status got better. Rick could not stand another surgery in the shape he was in. Now he was trying to wake up and was awake most of the days. Rick was so weak. He had so many pints of blood, it was unbelievable, sometimes four a day.

Four days later, Rick was septic again. He was running over 103 temperature. He had four different kinds of bacteria showing up in his urine, blood and lungs. Still on many antibiotics.

Four more days went by and Rick was much better. He was looking around and was able to lift his arms. That was quite an improvement. Abigale brought him two elastic bands to exercise his arms and a rubber ball to squeeze to help with some kind of strength in his hands and arms. Abigale told Rick when they left that day, she expected him to be able to throw the ball at her when she came back. Rick just looked at his parents and smiled.

Rick now had a valve for his trach so he could try to talk to them. He said he sounded like Wolf Man Jack. The family tried to talk to him a lot to try to keep his mind off things that were happening. Rick told them one day, "I wonder what that little girl was doing sitting on the foot of my bed last night". Abigale just looked at him and said, "I wonder". Rick started smiling and his eyes got great big. He had so many angels watching over him through this ordeal. When Rick first got sick, he watched the news all the time about the little Anthony girl. He was so worried about her. Maybe it was her? Abigale did believe in angels.

Rick just had not realized what all he had been through and probably just as well. Now he was getting addicted to Dilaudid, a stong IV pain medication. Every time he woke up, he was asking for it, along with Zofran, a nausea medicine. Abigale knew he had to be in pain, but sometimes she wondered if he just wanted to sleep through the whole ordeal and at one point he admitted that. Abigale tried to talk to him about the medication, but it didn't do any good. He would be fine when they would leave for home and when they would return, more medicines would be added. Very frustrating.

Everyone at home was concerned about Rick. They ask about him often. They would ask if he had cancer and that they were being told by Lucinda that he did and that he was not going to come home from the hospital. Where did all that come from?

When Rick was moved to the new ICU building, Abigale had later found in the records that an IV pump had "malfunctioned' and Rick was given 150 units of insulin. The family was not told anything about that incident. What else had happened to that poor man, who knows.

If Sam and Abigale were not working, they were either enroute to the hospital or at the hospital. When they were home, working, Abigale would call the nurses for updates before going to work and after work. Lucinda was at the place where she wouldn't tell the family anything, but once they were at the hospital, then leave for home, she would call and say they needed to come back right away. It got very tiring and stressful. We just kept on praying for strength and that God would help Rick get better and be able to come home soon.

A few days before Thanksgiving, Carie and Ariel went to visit Rick. Rick kept telling them he didn't feel right. The girls were standing by his bed and all of a sudden, Rick stopped breathing. Of course, Lucinda was gone. She always took off when the family came. Carie yelled for the nurse. The nurse turned around, looked at the monitor and said, "He's okay". He wasn't okay. Carie again said, "you need to come check him". Not quite that calmly. It wasn't until the alarms started sounding did she get up and come check Rick. Carie also had already text and tried to call Lucinda to return immediately to the room. Rick had already been down to CAT scan and back when Lucinda returned.

The night before Thanksgiving, Sam went to stay with Rick. Abigale and Carrie had to work Thanksgiving day and they were going the following Friday. When Sam arrived at the hospital, he called Abigale and told her something was not right with Rick. Abigale started with all the questions and found out Rick's blood pressure was 60/40. They also found out Rick had been getting 50mg of Fentanyl IV three times that day, every day since Sam and Abigale had left. Fentanyl is an IV medication used for pain, sedates a person and makes them forget. How convenient. How can a nurse, consiously, give a person so much medication and not feel guilty or worry about the well-being of the patient? And what kind of doctor would give such orders if he had even looked at the patient? Sam had a little discussion with the nurse and that medication was stopped. Rick was still getting the Dilaudid. A male nurse that night told Sam that he could tell if a patient was really in pain and Rick did not appear to be in that much pain. Rick did not have much medication thereafter and began to improve dramatically. Finally a nurse with some brains and common sense. On Thanksgiving day, Rick told Sam he wanted an "amp" drink. An energy drink promoted by Earnhardt, Jr, one of Rick's favorite nascar drivers. Thank God, he was beginning to be more like himself again. What a testimony he had to tell. He was bringing many people closer to the Lord with his determination and will to live.

Rick was like a yo-yo. Sam and Abigale would be with him, he would be fine. They would leave and it seemed like he would get worse again and they would get a phone call to return. Very suspicious. No one wants to believe terrible things, but something was not right. Sam and Abigale were reassured that the medications would be decreased. A new nurse would come on and it would start all over again, it seemed. By the end of the month, with many ups and downs, Rick had really improved. He was very alert, even smiling more and trying to laugh. Thank you Jesus!

Since Rick was improving so much, respiratory therapy began to do trach trials to see how long he could stay off the ventilator and breathe on his own. Rick now had yeast infections still in his lungs, in old IV sites and still in his blood. He had IV lines in his feet since they were having trouble finding veins that didn't have blood clots in them. The doctor's downsized Rick's trach allowing him to talk more with his valve. It was wonderful to hear his voice again, for the first time in months. Despite still being very sick, Rick would make jokes and smile. Such an inspiring person. What faith and strength. His favorite saying got to be, "Praise The Lord". The family began to tell him of all he had been through and how God had pulled him out of certain situations, been there at the right times and Rick would keep repeating, "Praise The Lord". Once again, Lucinda began to switch the valve and mess with it. She wouldn't wait for the nurses to do it. Abigale again prayed for strength and for the Lord to watch over Rick.

By that time, it was the first week of December and Rick was very awake and alert. He was doing quite well with the valve on his trach and could talk well. Most medications, except the Dilaudid were gone, he was off blood pressure medicines and his vital signs were good. He was on steroids now and they were helping him. The doctor's told the family Rick was free from infection for the first time in months. The surgeon told the family that Rick, more or less, was just going to have to live with his condition (fistula and not eating) until he could heal some and have another surgery to repair what had come undone from the abdominal surgery. The hospital staff had moved Rick to another room. He could see across the way, the ECMO building and the staff there had placed a sign in the window for Rick saying "Way to go Rick". It really gave Rick a boost. The doctor's started to talk of releasing Rick. They said they were going to release him to a nursing home in the same town as the hospital. Abigale told them Rick was not going to a nursing home and if she had to, she would quit work and take him home with her and take care of him. It upset Rick to hear Lucinda talk of a nursing home. Such a young man in a nursing home. Ridiculous! Abigale began to talk to the rehab unit at the hospital back home where she worked. They said they could not take him if he could not tolerate at least three hours of therapy a day. Rick had only been able to tolerate sitting up on the side of the bed for a few minutes. Abigale was willing to do anything to prevent Rick from having to go to a nursing home, especially in a strange town. She knew if he did, he wouldn't make it home alive or get stonger for another surgery. Some of the hospital staff was watching Lucinda closer. She began saying, "It's time to go, it's time to go".

In the middle of December, Rick had some more bleeding from his abdominal wound. The doctor's again held his blood thinners. The hospital staff placed a long term IV line. It looked like things were finally looking up. One of Abigale's sisters told her one of her favoite songs was "Even in the Valley, God is Good". So very, very true. God had brought Rick this far and there had to be a reason. The family was all so grateful, humble and praising God's name.

Abigale's heart was broken. Her hospital's rehab called and said they couldn't take Rick. They said he had to be walking first. Rick was depressed, wanted to come to his home town rehab. He ask Abigale if she could pull some strings. He must of thought his mom was more important than she really was, bless his heart. In the meantime, Rick was trying hard to work with physical therapy, but he had been down for almost four months and he was very weak. The next day, Rick took sixteen steps with the Lord's help. It was like the first steps he took when he was a baby. The family was overjoyed and Abigale felt so good going to work that morning, like a weight had been lifted. There was a reason. God was preparing her for more good news. Abigale's manager came to tell her the director and doctor of their rehab unit called and wanted to talk to her. She said they could use her office. The doctor and director came and they went into the manager's office. They began telling Abigale the reason they couldn't take Rick and why they refused to take him. Then they said due to some good news they had received that morning, they had changed their minds and was now going to take Rick. Dear God, thank you. Thank you for your blessings over and over. Abigale's son was coming home.

Rick's trach was removed on December 14th and Rick was released to his home town rehab the next day.

That morning when they rolled Rick into rehab on the ambulance cart, everyone was there waiting. Rick's hometown hospital was a pretty good sized hospital but everyone knows everyone else and it was like one big happy family. Everyone was so excited that Rick was there. As they started to pass the nurse's station, Abigale said, "Wait". She told Rick to look up on the wall. The words on the wall said, "The next step is home". Rick just smiled and said, "I can't wait".

Rick went to rehab with the TPN (IV nutrition), still an open abdominal wound, clots in most of his veins and still on Dilaudid and Zofran. The first thing rehab done was lab tests to check him out good. They found out he still had MRSA (a very resistant infecton to antibiotics) in his lungs and had been there since November. The family was so upset. The hospital had told the family Rick was infection free!

Abigale tried to talk to the doctors to see if they could maybe get Rick off the Dilaudid. Nothing seemed to help him like the Dilaudid. Rick finally admitted that he just wanted to sleep through this whole mess until he was well. Abigale couldn't imagine being in his shoes and all that he had been through.

Rehab was good. They started working with Rick on weights for his arms to get them stronger. It wasn't but a few days and they had him up in a chair. The abdominal wound was a hard thing to keep under control from leaking. The doctors was now letting him have liquids, but everything he took by mouth would come out his side through the fistula. The more he drank, the worse it would leak. Keeping the dressing dry was a constant battle. The floor nurses and wound care nurses did a wonderful job. They tried so many different things to see what worked best. Lucinda still would not leave things alone and the more the nurses ask her opinion (since she had seen it so much) the more she would mess with things. She was always in the nurse's way, they could hardly get to him. They never said a lot, they didn't want to offend her or Rick. It was just a rerun of the past. A few of the nurses had her pegged from day one, but the rest let her manipulate them.

The first thing on Lucinda's agenda was free meals. Somehow she managed to get three free meals a day. Why she didn't go home to eat is a question. She only lived a few minutes across town. Usually at the hospital, visitors had to pay for their meals, they were brought to the room, but Lucinda, somehow, got hers all free at the hospital. Abigale had heard since all this, that Lucinda complained about some of the food she got. The nerve! Abigale tried to talk to Lucinda about not eating in front of Rick. He had not had "real" food in over two months. She wouldn't listen, she would sit right down at the foot of his bed in front of him and eat. At one point, Abigale put a sign on the outside of the door asking that food not be taken into the room because the patient could not eat. Once Lucinda saw it, she complained to Rick and Rick asked Abigale to take it down. He said it didn't bother him for her to eat in front of him. Abigale just thought it would be a common courtesy not to eat in front of him.

Abigale, Sam and the family tried to get Lucinda to go back to work so Rick's insurance would not be jeopardized again. She refused. She said Rick wanted her there, but she wasn't there much. She was seen in the parking lot with her "girlfriend" whom she spent so much time with in her free room at the previous hospital.

It got to the point, when Abigale had to ask the nurses and staff to get Rick's ice chips he was given. Lucinda would go get ice chips and not come back for a while. The family begain, again to watch her. She would get the ice chips from the ice machine a few steps down the hall, go the other direction around the nuses station to the bathroom and eventually come back with the ice. This happened every time she went to get ice. The family suspected she was putting something in the ice. If Lucinda wasn't around, Rick would be fine. If she was, he would act different after taking the ice chips. Abigale began to dump out the ice chips Lucinda brought him and get new ones every time they visited. Rick was just too drowsy and something wasn't right.

Corella began to bring in big jugs of sweet tea to Rick. Rick wasn't allowed to have it, but she would sneak it in. Abigale didn't trust her either. Abigale finally ask the doctor if Rick could have it, to make it legal. Before all this started with Rick, Lucinda talked terrible about her mother They fought constantly. Now, it seemed, they were best of friends.

One day while Abigale was working, one of the nursing assistants she worked with got pulled to rehab to work. Mid afternoon, she came, sat down by Abigale and said, "Rick just walked fifty feet down the hall with the walker. Abigale just dropped everything and started to cry. Everyone, including the staff was rejoicing. Rick had touched so many lives with his strength and determination. Such an amazing man. Thank you Jesus!

Day by day, Rick got stronger. He was really hard to get on his feet and fell a couple times in the hallway while walking. He was determined and tried to push himself. He wanted to go home so bad. The rehab staff was wonderful and encouraged him so much. Finally, Rick's smile was returning, his attitude and mental status was improving.

Christmas was just around the corner. Abigle was hoping Rick would be home for Christmas, but he still wasn't strong enough. The family cancelled their Christmas get together and told Rick the family would celebrate Christmas once he was home along with all the other holidays and his birthday he had missed. Christmas Eve came and Abigale couldn't stand the thought of him spending it alone. Lucinda didn't offer to stay with him, so Abigale ask Rick if he wanted her to stay. Rick replied, "I would like that mom, if you would". Abigale remembered the satisfaction of being able to stay with him because now she realized it was his last Christmas. Abigale and Sam brought Rick a bag of goodies for Christmas. He was happy, but it was a sad time. They also brought Lucinda a bag, but she acted like she was in a hurry to leave so they took it back home.

Rick had many visitors. It was so good for him to be close to home where everyone could see him. It helped him mentally. That was a big part of his healing.

By the first of January, Rick was getting strong enough and doing so well, the doctors and staff were talking about Rick being released to home. By the middle of January, Rick was able to return home. The staff, physical therapists and nurses had done a trial run before releasing him. They took him home one day just to make sure he was able to get into the house and navigate well inside.

Leaving that day was a day Abigale would never forget. Rick was determined to walk out of rehab. The staff offered to take him to the car in a wheelchair, but Rick wanted to walk. Rehab was located on the second floor of the hospital. When Rick got ready to leave, everyone, family and staff was there to wish him the best. Before Rick got on the elevator, the staff gave him gifts and a certificate for completing rehab, along with big round of applause. It was so joyful. It was an unforgettable moment. Many were crying, including the family and staff. That is the way health care workers are supposed to care about their patients. Rick walked to the car and went home that day. The family was all there to help him get up the steps into the house. It was bittersweet knowing Rick was finally home, but was going to have to go through all this again when he went back to get the fistula repaired. Abigale just kept praying. The Lord had seen Rick through this far. They could only pray he could get back to normal again soon.

Once Rick returned home, he was more content. He could never have children, but his two dogs were like his children. They wouldn't leave his side. That made Abigale a little uneasy due to all Rick's equipment he had, but they were all happy and together once again. One of the nurses from rehab and the wound care nurses from the hospital came to check on Rick on their own time. Such compassion.

Things got back to normal, as could be, with the situation the way it was. Abigale and the family would go by to check on Rick often and do what they could do for him. Abigale and Carie had offered to go by to give Rick his medication, but the home health care let Lucinda give it. Abigale was upset because she didn't think an unqualified person should be administering medication, especially IV narcotics. Mainly, Rick wasn't doing much of anything at all except lying in bed, watching TV, taking Dilaudid and Zofran with no exercise. He had so many bags to carry around with him when he got up to go to the bathroom, he thought it was hardly worth getting up.

Abigale, rehab and home health care had shown Lucinda how to do the sterile dressing changes, but it didn't do any good. With Rick's dogs on the bed with him all the time, Abigale tried to express the importance of how to be as sterile as possible due to the open wound Rick still had and all the problems he had with infection. One day, Abigale stopped by after work to check on Rick. He needed a dressing change. Lucinda wouldn't let Abigale change it. She yelled for Winnie to come help. Winnie came in and started opening the sterile bandages and throwing them on the bed. Lucinda picked them up and placed them in Rick's open wound. Abigale cringed and ask them not to do that, but it was like they were doing it on purpose and did it anyway. They were determined to do the opposite of what Abigale ask. Rick was so drugged, he had no clue what they were doing.

Another day while Abigale was there checking on Rick, he said he needed pain medication. Abigale got it ready and started giving it slowly like it is supposed to be given. Rick said, "Mom, just shoot it in like Lucinda does". She explained it was supposed to be given slowly and he said it didn't help as much that way. He was addicted big time and Lucinda wasn't helping matters any.

Lucinda finally made plans to go back to work. Her employer was threatening her with her job and for insurance sake, she decided to go back. She went back and the first day she worked, Rick told Abigale that Lucinda came home, sat down on the opposite side of the bed and started crying because her feet hurt. Rick said he got up, packed up his IV bags, oxygen, drainage cannister and all his equipment to the other side of the bed to comfort Lucinda. She never went back to work again. She got another leave of absence to stay home with Rick.

This went on for a couple months. When Rick had to go back to follow up with the surgeon, they began to talk about scheduling him for a repair surgery. By this time, Rick and the family had talked about not ever going back to that hospital or doctor. Rick was afraid to go back after all that had happened. Even though Rick had plans not to go back, he went for his appointment anyway. Rick's abdominal would, miraculously was healing some, closing some, but still leaking. The doctor seemed impressed and said something to Lucinda about being a good nurse. She, like many times before said, "I am a nurse, all I need is the terminology". The doctor looked at Abigale and Abigale told him, "We all know it takes a whole lot more that that". He agreed and it made Lucinda mad. Before this, she was still determined Rick was going to return to that same hospital, but now she did an opposite turn a round. She didn't want him to go back there and ageed he should go somewhere else if they could find a doctor willing to take on such a mess.

Sam's cousin who had the multiple organ transplant had been keeping up on Rick's progress. When he heard Rick was not wanting to go back to that hospital, he offered to talk to his doctor at another hospital three hours from where Rick lived. He did just that and arrangements were made to go see a new doctor and surgeon. Abigale had her doubts that any doctor would want to touch such a dificult problem, but it was sure worth a try for Rick's sake.

In February, Rick went to see the new doctor. He ask Abigale and Sam to go with them and Ariel decided to go and drive. When they pulled into the parking lot, it was full except for some handicap parking areas. Ariel made several turns around the parking lot and finally Lucinda pulled out a handicap parking tag and tried to give it to Ariel. Unbelievale! Ariel just found a place to park and we went in. It was an very stressful day for Rick. The long ride and very emotional. Before the doctor came into the office, Rick needed to go to the bathroom. Lucinda went with him. When they came out, Abigale could tell Rick had been medicated. By the time the doctor came in, Rick was in such an emotional state, he couldn't sit still. He was pacing back and forth, crying and just wouldn't sit down. The doctor just kept looking at them all and started to ask questions. He ask Lucinda how they had been doing at home. She said, "We read our bibles and pray". What a comment. She tried to put on such a show. The doctor explained to Rick that he would admit him to that hospital and do a workup, have a new surgeon see him and see what they could do about getting him fixed up. God is good! Now they needed to get Rick calmed down from being over medicated.

He ended up in the local hospital a week before he was supposed to go to the new hospital with a staph infection in his IV line.

Around the first of March, Rick was admitted to the new hospital for a workup and to see the new surgeon. Constant prayers.

Rick was admitted to the new hospital. Before Rick was even admitted, Lucinda supposedly had a low blood sugar attack. The nurses were running around, carrying her drink, worrying about her and not once did anyone see what her sugar really was. She was gettng all the attention and there was Rick lying in the bed, worrying about her. This happened each time they went to a new place.

The doctor Rick had seen in the office previously came in and talked with Rick, ran a lot of tests, gave him encouragement and said the surgeon would be seeing him tomorrow. The next morning, the new surgeon came in and looked at Rick. He was a very stern man, very serious looking and had a team of other doctor's and students walking behind him. It was obvious, he was very intelligent. The doctor looked at Rick, examined his belly and ask, "Are you tired of leaking?" Rick said, "Yes I sure am". The surgeon ask, "Are you hungry?' Rick replied "Yes". By this time Rick was getting teary eyed. The surgeon ask, "What would you like to eat?" Rick replied, "McDonalds". The doctor ask, "What would you like from McDonalds?" Rick said, "Big Mac". That cut the ice and by that time, everyone had tears streaming down their faces. Rick was crying too and ask the surgeon, "Can you fix me?". The surgeon said, "I'm sure gonna try". This man was sent from God. The surgeon told them all that the PICC line Rick had, was actually a midline, not as long as a PICC line and would not be suitable for what was ahead for Rick. It also was curled up inside his arm and should not have been getting TPN through it. Rick was scheduled for Rick to have a real PICC line inserted.

By the following Friday, Rick had a real PICC line, the fistula had been bridged off and a new feeding tube in his stomach to help build up his nutrition for the impending surgery scheduled in a couple weeks. The surgeon said Rick would have a better quality of life until the repair surgery took place. Abigale loved this surgeon. All of everyone's prayers were being answered. God surely does listen.

Lucinda was only concerned, again about getting a free room, free parking and free meals. She didn't like it there because none of that was possible. She would just have to stay in Rick's room in the chair. She ask for a recliner, but they told her if one was available they would get it for her. Abigale noticed Lucinda checking out all the boxes on the wall that held the syringes for the nurses. Abigale had a talk with one of the nurses and the syringes were taken out of the room.

By the next morning, the tube that had just been placed in Rick's belly "fell out". The feedings had to be stopped and now it would be Monday before they could fix it.

Rick saw many doctor's while he was there. They were checking him out well. They told him there was a chance he might loose his entire pancreas. Rick was very upset and devastated. So much going on and so stressful for him. He was an emotional wreck to say the least. Part of the reason, Abigale thought, was withdrawal from all the Dilaudid he had been getting at home and who knows what else. Rick had a huge dose of Ativan for his nerves that knocked him out. He did get some much needed rest. After waking up the next morning, Rick was so depressed. Abigale, Sam and Rick talked of planning a trip to Daytona for the nascar race that summer. Abigale told him to try to think of positive things and he was soon smiling. Rick's cousin came to visit him and that helped his spirits. His cousin was a fine young lady who lived in the town where the hospital was. Ironically, when Rick was a small child, he had a problem with biting. He never bit anyone except this certain cousin. Abigale figured he liked her and wanted her attention and he sure got it.

By the end of the week, Rick still seemed depressed. Abigale ask him what he could say good about that day. Rick replied, "Everything got done!" By the end of the day, Rick was smiling and not acting so depressed. Abigale ask him again about what was positive. Rick said, "Daytona next summer". Abigale said, "Yes, warm weather and sunny beaches". Rick said, "Girls in bikinis". Everyone was laughing except Lucinda. Rick looked at Lucinda and said, "Just kidding". Abigale said, "Lucinda would probably wear a bikini for you if you ask her too". Rick replied, "That would be like me wearing a speedo". Everyone howled, except for Lucinda. At this time we only wanted Rick to be smiling and joking as he was.

Rick returned home with a real PICC line, feeding tube, TPN and oxygen. The medical doctor discussed with Rick things he could do to prepare for the next surgery scheduled the first week of April. He wanted Rick to walk as much as possible and work with an incentive spirometry to exercise his lungs. He even gave Rick a big hug before he left. Wow, such compassion.

The family again took turns going by Rick's house to help him walk around the block, giving him encouragement, and trying to help in any way they could. Rick was now at 205 pounds. He had went into the first hospital weighing 260 pounds. What a way to loose weight. Rick was not home two days until two of the stitches holding his feeding tube got "pulled" out. So frustrating.

In the middle of March, Rick got to taste a couple bites of Dairy Queen ice cream. He could only take a couple bites, but at least he got to taste some real food. Everyone visited, trying to keep his spirits up. Dale would take his daughters by to see Rick. Rick loved them so much. The baby didn't quite know what to think of all Rick's tubes, but she did remember his phone. Rick used to let her play with it all the time.

After another appointment with the impending surgeon at the end of March, everyone was so encouraged. The doctor's kept patting Rick on the back, telling him what a good job he was doing. They told Rick they did not need to remove the pancreas, and the surgery was gonna take six hours. After the appontment, they were leaving, Rick began to cry and said, "Thank You Lord". It was the Lord who led him to that hospital and those wonderful doctor's

Three days later, Abigale tried to call Rick's house but didn't get an answer. She went to Rick's house and Lucinda was gone. Rick was sleeping. After Lucinda got home, Abigale went home. Rick called to tell Abigale he had been running a temperature. Rick called his primary care physician. They did some blood cultures and a chest x-ray. Rick was once again admitted to the local hospital for staph infection in his PICC line and was put on antibiotics. The doctors from the most recent hospital had been keeping in contact with Rick's local physician. They told the primary doctor, Rick might have to stay in the hospital until his surgery was scheduled. Rick didn't want that, but it might be necessary to keep him stay infection free. After a couple days in the hospital, Rick was so much better. Laughing, talking and cracking jokes. One of the wound care nurses had worked previously with the new impending surgeon and talked with Rick about how good he was. That also made Rick feel better. Rick was now talking about getting better and wanting to look for a good fishing spot. Rick loved to fish as did his brother Dale.

Against Abigale's better judgement, the doctor's released Rick to go home the first of April. Easter Sunday, Abigale and Sam had all the kids and families for dinner. Rick still couldn't eat anything except for liquids. He said he liked mushroom soup, so Abigale strained some mushroom soup and made him a milkshake. He took very little of it, but at least he had some sort of an Easter dinner.

With all the friction between Lucinda and Rick's family, Abigale and Sam decided to have a talk with Rick and Lucinda before the surgery. They didn't want Rick to worry about anything except getting well. They were very honest, told them both about all the things that had happened and how they felt. Of course, Lucinda denied most of what they knew she had done. Sam told them, "God knows our hearts". Rick said, "Yes" and Lucinda said, "God knows but we don't know". We were determined to get along with her for Rick's sake.

The first week of April, Rick was feeling pretty good. Lucinda took him shopping. Abigale was not real happy about him going into stores, due to being afraid he would catch another bug and get sick. Surgery was scheduled in less than a week. He also still had all those tubes hanging from him. I'm sure he got some stares and Lucinda got lots of sympathy. Little did Abigale know, Rick and Lucinda had also made some funeral arrangements for Rick.

Before Rick went into the hospital, he decided he wanted to make Abigale his power of attorney. That was a big relief to Abigale. That way, decisions could not be made to jeopardize Rick's living or dying.

By the end of the first week in April, Sam and Abigale took their camper to a campsite within ten minutes from where Rick would be having his surgery. Everyone was praying so hard for this surgery to go smoothly and for Rick to be able to get back to living a normal life. He was very stressed, anxious and nervous. He had every right to be.

Early on the morning of April 9th, Rick went into surgery after a gathering of the entire family. Rick's minister and some of the church people were there to be with them. Rick expressed how afraid he was and the minister's prayer before going into surgery helped calm him down. Everyone was very nervous and anxious, but they couldn't let Rick know how they felt. A friend of Abigale's had brought her a prayer cloth from her church for Rick. Abigale taped it to Rick's foot and left it there. Rick went into surgery.

The surgery went amazingly well. The surgeon came out into the waiting room a few hours later. Everyone was all on edge and on the edge of their seats waiting to hear the news. The surgeon was so calm and started explaining that he had repaired a hernia, removed the fistula and Rick was doing fine. Abigale ask if Rick was on a ventilator. The surgeon said he was, but they probably would take him off before he left the recovery room. Abigale and her family were all so relieved and so thankful that God had worked another miracle they all just broke down and started crying and hugged each other. They could not thank this surgeon enough. He was a man sent from God. Rick had a tube in his nose, oxygen, two drains in his stomach and a feeding tube in his stomach in case he needed it later for nutrition.

When the family got to see Rick after recovery, he was awake, talking and also praising the Lord. He was laughing, joking and smiling ear to ear. What a day to rejoice. Rick was finally, once again back on the road to recovery and the family was all so relieved. Everyone was so happy. The news was once again sent out all over and prayer chains continued.

The day after surgery, Rick was able to sit up in the chair twice that day. His blood pressure was running a little low, but he was doing fine. Rick even was able to watch the Nascar race that was on TV that day. By night fall, Rick was having some congestion and the doctor started him on some breathing treatments which helped. By the next day, Rick had to get two pints of blood which also helped his breathing. He sat up again in the chair and the doctor told the family that Rick was doing fine. One more day on critical care and he could probably be moved to another room on the regular surgery floor. Amazing and unbelievable. Rick was finally getting some well deserved rest after all he had been through. It had been another great day for Rick. When he started passing gas, have a bowel movement, he could get that tube out of his nose and start to eat. He had not eaten "real food" in over six months. Three days after sugery, Rick was moved to a regular surgery floor.

The next day, Rick's congestion got worse, his heart rate was running in the 150's and stayed there for over six hours. The staff worked diligently with Rick all day to try to get rid of the fluid overload he was in. That evening, Rick was moved back to critical care and had to, once again, be placed back on the ventilator. When Abigale, Lucinda, Sam and the family went to the critical care room, the staff was standing all around Rick preparing to place him back on the ventilator. Abigale ask if she could talk to Rick and they let her in the room. Rick was scared. Abigale felt so bad for him. She told him, "Rick they need to do this to get you over this hump". Rick looked at Abigale and said, "Okay, Mom, I love you guys". Abigale told Rick she loved him to. So heartbreaking. The staff placed Rick back on the ventilator, was able to clean out his lungs and Rick was able to rest comfortably. The doctor was hoping Rick would be able to come off the ventilator in just a day or two. Prayers were, once again, going out all over.

Abigale and Sam arrived at the hospital the next morning and entered Rick's room. The male nurse never spoke one word to them. He went to the door, yelled for help and Rick was again coded for a respiratory arrest. Devastating. Rick was once again critically ill. The doctor placed Rick on a special bed. It strapped him in, top and bottom and he was rocked back and forth continuously on his stomach. This was to help his lungs recover. All that could be seen was Rick's arms, his shoulders and a small portion of his face. They would turn him on his back about every four hours, remove the padding and check out his skin, tubes and see how he did on his back. Rick's face got so swollen, he was unrecognizable. The family was assured this was normal due to him lying on his stomach all the time.

Abigale's oldest sister, her sister's daughter and her minister, Rick's minister, Lucinda and her mother and Lucinda's aunt and uncle were all there. Everyone took turns staying in the room with Rick. Abigale's niece kept them all fed and prayers were going out everywhere.

As Abigale was standing by Rick's bedside, he rocked towards her. She looked at Rick's right shoulder blade and there was a perfect pink heart that would come and disappear, come and disappear. Abigale started crying and told Sam and the kids to come see. As they were all standing there, looking at the heart, they knew it was God's way of telling them Rick was going to be alright.

The doctor's were puzzled as to why Rick had gotten sick again. They just couldn't figure out what had gone wrong. They did blood cultures. Rick also had to be placed on dialysis because his kidney function was not doing well. His white blood count was also elevated again. The fear of infection, once again, was there. The doctor wanted to do a CAT scan on Rick's stomach, but he was not well enough to be moved off the special bed long enough.

Rick slowly began to improve and the doctor's were talking of moving him off the special bed to another special bed that kept him on his back and turned him side to side to help distribute oxygen. That bed did not help him as much and he had to be put back on the other bed. They began to decrease the ventilator settings. By this time, the family had grown to love one special female nurse who kept very good care of Rick. She worked diligently with him and brought him out of several crisis. The doctor's were saying that Rick would have to stay on dialysis until he came off the ventilator.

By the middle of the month, Rick was once again, improving. The family was convinced it was due to the good nursing care he had received. Rick had not had a bad nurse since he had been there, until 7PM that evening.

When Rick had to be turned, there would be two nurses, one at each end to watch the tubes for safety. That evening, a different male nurse came in, went about his duties without speaking to any of the family. There were five family members sitting there. The nurse appeared as if he was going to turn Rick. Abigale questioned him about getting a second nurse. He ignored her and started to turn Rick. All of a sudden, fluid started to splatter all over the floor. Abigale jumped up, told the nurse something was wrong and Rick began to make a gurgling noise. Rick's oxygen saturation began to fall. The nurse had left the room and was on the phone outside the room. Carie ran to the door to ask the nurse if he was going to do anything because his sats were in the sixties. When he ignored her, she ran down the hall and yelled for help and grabbed a doctor. Sure enough, Rick's nasogastric tube and ventilator tubes had been pulled out. He had to be sedated to replace them. Abigale was furious. The doctor came to the doorway after Rick was situated and told Abigale, "Yes the ET tube had migrated out". Migrated out? No, it was pulled out. Now here Rick was back to square one. How much more was he going to have to go through? Abigale requested that the nurse not be back in Rick's room and they replaced him with another nurse.

That night, Lucinda was going to stay at Rick's bedside until Abigale relieved her at 4AM. There were only a couple chairs in the room. The staff had taken out the big couch in order to make room for all the equipment and in case they had another emergency, they would have room to get to Rick. Lucinda left to get some rest. As Abigale just got sat down in Rick's room, it was time to turn him. The nurse who caused the damage earlier waltzed into the room to help. Abigale ask him what he was doing. She was beside herself. The nurse replied, "I am helping turn him". Abigale told him, "No you're not. We ask that you not be in this room again." The nurse that had taken over told Abigale, "If you want to be upset with someone, be upset with me, I ask him to help". After some investigation, Abigale found out that he had been helping all night while Lucinda was in the room and she had not said a word. Did she not care about Rick's safety? It seemed like she made a point of doing the opposite of what Abigale thought best. That should have been common sense after what had occurred earlier.

Abigale's older sister had since returned home, but with all the problems with Rick, she had returned to be with the family and help out. The next day Rick had another wonderful nurse. He was a male nurse, young and very determined to take very good care of Rick. He worked wonders with Rick after all that had happened the day before. Vent settings were lower, kidneys began working well and Jim told us that if Rick continued to do so well, he would be able to go for that CAT scan the doctors had been wanting to do to check the surgery to make sure things were as they should be.

Sam's sister, her husband and Sam's cousin had come to visit. Little did Sam and Abigale know, Lucinda had began to solicit money from Sam's family as well.

Two days later, Rick was able to go down for the CAT scan. It was found that he had a leak in his stomach at the surgical site. The doctor said they hoped they could put in a drain and it would heal on it's own. Of course, more prayer requests went out to that effect.

The next day, Rick was again showing improvement. Sam and Abigale went to the camper for the first time in days to try to get some rest and get cleaned up. They had not thought about resting or getting cleaned up with all that had happened. All they cared about Rick. Showering was Lucinda's first priority every morning, no matter what was going on. "When Sam and Abigale returned the next morning, Lucinda had talked the staff into taking the couch back into the room. "Her back hurt from sitting in those chairs." The swelling was almost gone from Rick's face. He was beginning to look like Rick again. It was another day with a bad nurse. Rick never did well when he had a bad nurse. The nurse spent little time in Rick's room and when he went to give Rick insulin, he just walked into the room, didn't say a word and shot the needle into Rick's arm. Abigale told Rick, even though he was unconcious, "I think that was your insulin shot". The nurse just walked out of the room without saying a word. No improvement that day for sure. Rick was getting blood pressure medication to keep his blood pressure up, Ativan, Dilaudid, heart medications, IV nutrition, antibiotics, insulin and bicarb. The doctor's were discussing taking him down to place a drain tube where they had discovered the leak at the surgical site.

Over the next few days, the favorite female nurse was back and the family could relax because they knew Rick would be well taken care of. Sam's aunt and her son who had been through a multiple organ transplant at the same hospital came to visit. Everyone was calling daily and praying.

In two days, Rick had improved dramatically. Everyone was elated. One of the female doctor's that told the family a few days before there was no hope came in that morning all smiles to report things were good and Rick had improved. Abigale knew God had his arms around Rick and prayers continued. How can some people believe there is no God when there had been so many miracles? Ariel and Carie came to stay with Rick the weekend so Sam and Abigale could return home and work a couple days. Saturday the girls had called so excited to tell Sam and Abigale that the labs were much improved and Rick had his eyes open and was trying to move on his own. A chest tube and drain tube had been removed. The good news was sent out to everyone. They were praising and thanking the Lord all over the place.

Sam and Abigale made it through two days of work and returned to the hospital on Monday so Carie and Ariel could go home to their families and jobs. Over the next few days, Rick continued to improve, went for another CAT scan and the doctor's were talking about putting in a different trach to help him get off the vent a little easier. The CAT scan showed two pockets of fluid or maybe one that had run into another area. The sludge they had seen earlier had turned to fluid which would make it easier to drain. God does answer prayers! The doctor's did not have to even put in a drain because the surgeon said it looked like old blood. Praise the Lord! Ventilator settings improved. Rick was now on only intermittent dialysis instead of continuous. He had his eyes open more and when the monitors would go off, he would shake his head "No". That was a good sign. He was more alert.

Sam and Abigale left, once again for three days to go home to work. Lucinda started back to her old tricks, messing with tubes while talking on her cell phone, not washing her hands. Corella was also back which made Abigale nervous. Abigale could only pray that God would continue to hold Rick in his arms and watch over him. God is the great physician. Winnie, Rick's stepdaughter also had some news. She was pregnant. She was waiting to tell Rick when he was more alert and if it was a boy, they were going to name him after Rick. He would be thrilled. He loved kids.

Sam and Abigale never made it to work. They got a call at 3AM telling them Rick was having trouble breathing and running a temperature. Unbelievable, it seemed like he would do so well, they would leave and down he would go again. They returned to the hospital. Abigale noticed a green stain in Rick's beard. She ask the nurse if Rick had been vomiting and she replied, "Not today. He vomited last night and you were sitting right there on the couch". Abigale replied, "No I was not and I had no idea he had vomited." Abigale feared Rick would aspirate again. He still had a nasogastric tube and the fluid in the tube was fluctuating as he breathed. He shouldn't be nauseated with that tube in, let alone vomit. She ask the nurse to check the placement of the tube. She said it was okay. Now here Rick was again . . . low blood pressure, high pulse, blood gases, increased ventilator settings, temperature of 101.4 and struggling to breathe. Rick had to be put back on the rotating bed and had to have another dialysis catheter placed. Two days later he began to improve again. No blood pressure medication at all now. He had to have more blood. He had graduated to two hours on his back and two hours on his belly rotating back and forth.

Rick's respiratory status was stable. Sam and Abigale again tried to go home to work again. They no more got in their back door and the phone rang. It was their favorite nurse telling them that they needed to return. Rick was deteriorating fast. They jumped back into the car and started back to the hospital. Enroute, the nurse called them twice to update them on Rick's condition. When Sam and Abigale arrived, Rick was stabilizing, but his white blood count was 60 when it should be around 8-10. Lucinda and her aunt were sitting on the couch in the room talking and laughing. Rick was critical again. He was septic again. He was started on another antibiotic that cost $3800 per dose, as Lucinda said, and he was getting it four times a day. Whatever it took. Prayers were continuing all over the world by now. By that afternoon, Rick's white blood count was down to 21. His chest x-ray was better, could hear air moving through his lungs and was able to go back down for another CAT scan. The CAT showed tiny abcesses in his liver caused from the IV nutrition. Urine output at this time was zero, he needed fluid, but with his lung problems, he was between a rock and a hard place about getting fluids to take care of that. He was still on continuous dialysis again. By this time, Lucinda had ask for a brain wave monitor to check for brain dead as his living will stated. She was on that brain dead kick now. The nurses would try to clean out his mouth with swabs and he would clamp down on the swabs. They talked of doing "sneak attacks". Ariel's husband would get down close to Rick's ear and sing the Rocky Balboa song and Rick's brain waves would just dance. Rick was probably laughing like crazy inside.

As things started to improve, once again, everyone was praying for Rick to have a bowel movement. I'm sure God didn't think it was a bunch of sick people to pray for such a thing considering the circumstances. By this time the staff was doing all they could do to prevent further infection. They kept the IV lines changed routinely. One nurse had a boyfriend who also worked at the hospital and when she was off, she would have her boyfriend check on Rick for her. They were becoming just like family.

The first week of May, Rick was put back on the bed that kept him on his back and rotated his shoulders back and forth. It would wake him up frequently. His bowels finally started to move and the family rejoiced. Good sign things were moving through. So many caring people, calling and praying for Rick. All of the family's co-workers and people they didn't even know were calling and checking on his progress. Carie's little girl found a little bear and she had Carie bring it to Rick. She wanted him to have it, she missed him. It was so cute because it was a Christmas bear, but that surely didn't matter.

One week later, Rick had improved to a point, the doctor's were going to do trach trials off the ventilator. The surgeon had put in a drain where the fistula had returned in his stomach and said there was a 80% chance it would heal on it's own. The catheter had been removed from his bladder, just another source of infection. His kidneys were not producing any urine, but they said they would work on that when his abdomen got straightened out. Rick was beginning to mouth words and shake his head yes and no to questions. Sam and Abigale were disturbed when Rick had bowel movement come out his side where the fistula was. Sam and Abigale realized they had to be more specific about their prayers. They began to pray and ask everyone else to pray for bowel movements and to come out the correct location. Rick was amazing everyone with his progress. The surgeon told Rick he was one strong man. The prayer cloth on Rick's foot got soiled one day when our favorite nurse was there. She went home and made another and prayed over it. She brought it back the next day and taped it back on his foot. Abigale had also found out that the one got soiled. Her friend's church had made Rick another. Now he had one taped to each foot. Most people knew what they were but some would just look at them and ask what they were. When they found out what they were for, they would just look at Rick and it seemed like something would click. You could tell by the look on their faces that they then realized why he was still here. The doctor's were talking about putting Rick on a regular bed now.

The next morning, Abigale walked into Rick's room. He winked at her. Her heart melted. Rick was back, praise the Lord, again!!

Since Rick was again doing well, Sam and Abigale went home to work a couple more days. The second day they were home, Lucinda called saying Rick's heart rate was dropping into the 20's and 30's. The doctor thought maybe the nasogastric tube in his nose was making him gag, causing his heart rate to drop. It was removed. Later that day, Rick started to vomit. Rick had three bronchosopies that day to check for aspiration. The tube had to be put down again. Now Rick was lipping words, "I want a drink". This broke Abigale's heart but at least he was alert enough to ask. The chest x-ray showed possible pneumonia. Dear God, not again!

The next day, Rick was sitting up in the cardio chair. He was alert, awake and mouthing words. The doctors were optimistic about the drainage coming from his side. They told the family they expected the fistula to heal on it's own. Rick had to have a better dialysis catheter placed. They found another blood clot in his right subclavian vein. They were running out of places to place necessary lines. They were saying another 6-8 weeks of recovery. At least they were talking recovery. Discussions were beginning about Rick going back to the rehab once again in his hometown. Everyone was so excited and wanted him close to home. They had done such a wonderful job with him the first time, we knew it would be good for him, mentally and physically.

Rick was able to get up in the cardio chair every day. The nurses would take him out on the balcony. He loved that fresh air, but it tired him out so much. He was still very weak. By this time, Sam and Abigale were working and going to the hospital on their days off. They began not to tell Lucinda when they were coming because they had heard rumors that she was leaving Rick alone when they weren't there.

By May 20th, Rick was sick again. He mouthed words, "Help me". He was septic again. Unbelievable. He had to get more blood transfusions and more fluid boluses. His immune system was so low, he couldn't fight off infections. His white blood count was again back up into the forties. More blood cultures and all lines were again changed as well as they could be. Abigale felt so helpless and everyone just wanted to do anything they could do to help. Dale and Winnie's boyfriend had been spending time fishing to catch enough fish for the big fish fry Rick wanted to have when he got home. Now the prayers were the same as they had been all the months before. Praying specifically for no more infections, no more bleeding, lungs to stay good, fistula to heal and bowels and kidneys to function properly. That should cover it all. It was all turned over to the Lord to handle.

The nasogastric tube was irritating Rick's stomach, causing bleeding so the surgeon ordered it to be taken out. The blood thinner was also stopped. Abigale reminded them that Rick had the same problem at the other hospital with his sensitivity to medications. It was hard to know what to do with all the clots he had. Things began to improve again. Rick's white blood count returned to normal, blood gases and lungs were improving again and physical therapy began to do range of motion on his arms and legs for strengthening. Rick had not been out of bed for over a month. He was stiff and very weak. His bowels were moving and he was not using much pain medication.

The surgeon scheduled a family meeting. Everyone was there. Everyone was apprehensive as to what he had to say. The meeting went well. The doctor's were concerned because they were running out of places to put lines due to so many blood clots. Rick didn't like the physical therapy but it was necessary. Dialysis was intermittent now and the doctor decided to use heparin instead of another blood thinner because it was easier on his kidneys.

The last day of the month, Sam and Abigale returned home to work. Lucinda called to say Rick was again having trouble. He was breathing fast, high heart rate and blood count was up again. Abigale knew he was getting septic again. By this time they knew all the signs. It had happened so many times and how Rick reacted.

The next day, Rick was still very sick. He had been off the ventilator 48 hours, but with this recent bout of infection, more blood, more fluids and more congestion in his lungs, he had to be put back on the ventilator so he could get some rest. That night Rick had his favorite male nurse. He took such good care of him. The first thing Jim would do was to wash down everything with sanitizor. Rick felt so at ease with him. By early morning, Rick's white blood count was back to normal. Rick went down for a scope on his stomach. The surgeon came in later to tell the family, they found a perforation in his stomach. The only way to fix it was surgery. Abigale knew Rick was in no condition for another surgery but there was no other choice. The surgeon said he didn't know if Rick could survive the surgery. Everyone was so nervous and scared, but we couldn't let Rick see that. The surgeon also said Rick needed to get some good rest that night. When Sam, Abigale and Rick's siblings were leaving, Lucinda, Corella, Winnie, her boyfriend and Lucinda's brothers were entering the room. Hopefully, they wouldn't stay long so Rick could rest.

The next morning with the impending surgery, everyone was there. Still very worried, they couldn't let Rick know. He knew what the surgeon was saying, that he may not come out of surgery alive. Rick told us, "I am not afraid, God has me in his arms". Abigale was so happy to hear Rick say this. Everyone stayed at Rick's bedside except for Lucinda and her family. They were in the waiting room. It was so hard to understand why she wasn't by Rick's side when this could be the last time they could talk to him, hug him, hold him in their arms and let him know how much they all loved him. Carie had brought her CD player and played Rick's favorite songs by Chris Tomlinson. They talked, laughed, cried and spoke their inner feelings. Rick was not afraid. When the time came for Rick to be taken to surgery, everyone gathered at Rick's bedside along with some of the nurses, some who were not even taking care of him that day. Lucinda's aunt said, "I think we are all here". Abigale said, "No, we are waiting on our son-in-law". About that time, Rick's dialysis machine started making a loud beeping noise. Rick's minister, who was sitting in his wheelchair holding Rick's hand said, "Did I win a prize? When you get well Rick, I give you permission to go to Vegas, but no girly shows". That broke the ice and everyone laughed including Rick. Ariel's husband arrived and Rick's minister said a prayer for Rick and his surgery. Everyone except for Lucinda, Sam, Abigale and Rick's siblings went on to the waiting room. A man from Rick's church walked with Lucinda. When we got to the elevator, Abigale ask Sam if he would say a prayer. Before Sam could say the prayer, the man with Lucinda made a mad dash to Rick's cart, grabbed his hand, said "I am from the church" and started praying. Rick was staring at Abigale, still looking her in the eyes when they rolled him into the elevator. Abigale mouthed the words, "I love you". Everyone went to the waiting room to wait. They expected to be there a while. Sam, Abigale, Carie, Ariel and Dale sat in one corner. The minister, Lucinda, Corella sat in the other corner. Abigale needed quiet time. She did not want to socialize. She finally broke down, telling her family that if Rick didn't survive, they would probably have to bury her along side him. She realized later she shouldn't have said such a thing. It was so hard on all of them and they didn't need any more worry. Lucinda and her mother, on the other hand, were laughing, talking and acting like it was just another day. Abigale didn't understand. The minister came over to Abigale to see if she was alright. She told him she was okay and needed to break down every now and then.

They settled in to what they expected to be a long wait. After about an hour, the doors opened, the surgeon came walking through and Abigale's heart sank. She could only think, Rick was gone. As the surgeon walked towards Abigale and her family, Corella yelled, "the family is over here". The surgeon continued to walk toward Abigale's corner. He looked at the family, shook his head and said, "all I had to do was put in a drain tube". He started smiling. They were all so relieved. They were rejoicing, thanking Jesus again. By that time, Lucinda and her mother were standing there. The look on their faces were for a Kodak moment. They looked so disappointed. When Rick returned to his room, he was laughing and so happy. Abigale told Rick, "anyone who thinks there is no God, is so lost". Rick was living proof and never ceased to amaze everyone.

The next morning, the surgeon came in and nicknamed Rick, Lazurus. Everyone was so amazed at how much he had been through and how much he had come through. Still the sweet, smiling, gentle person he always was. Never cross or in a bad mood, it seemed. Rick began, again, to improve. He was more alert and doing trach trials. He looked and acted so much better.

By the second week in June, Rick was septic again. As Abigale drove to work that morning, a female doctor called her, telling her Rick was very sick and they had done all they could do for him. Abigale told her, "Rick is a fighter and they were not about to give up on him". That afternoon Abigale talked to the infection control doctor. He told Abigale Rick had pseudomonas in his lungs, belly and blood. He also had the acineobactor infection in his lungs again. Abigale ask him about the isolation and tried to talk with him about Lucinda messing with tubes, Rick's belly, not washing her hands and not following isolation guidelines. She ask him if the isolation was for Rick or for everyone else. He said, "for everyone else". Abigale told him, "don't you think it is time everyone started worrying about Rick's safety?" The doctor made no reply. Rick ended up back on blood pressure medication to keep up his low blood pressure and was back on continuous dialysis. Dialysis was one of Rick's biggest fears before he went to surgery. He had a friend who was a dialysis patient and he had passed away shortly before Rick had his first surgery. Abigale thought the only way to protect Rick was to put him in a bubble.

Another bad bout of infection was over and Rick was again improving. He was able to be off the vent, sit up in the cardio chair, go out to the balcony again and enjoy the weather. He was more alert, had his days of being sad, scared, had good days and bad days. He deserved his feelings. Abigale and Sam kept telling Rick that God had a plan for him. It was going to be wonderful for him to tell his testimony, to win more souls for the Lord. He had already touched so many lives.

By the next week, the drain the surgeon had put in Rick's stomach had "fell" out. Rick was taken back down to CAT scan to see if the doctor could replace the tube. They also attempted to put in more permanent lines for dialysis, but was unable to do so due to so many blood clots. Rick had ask the doctor in radiology to please not let him die. That was the first time Rick had mentioned it to any doctor. Abigale got a call at work that day from Rick. He had his talk valve on. Abigale would never be able to forget the sound of his voice. She had not heard him actually speak in months. Rick never lost his sense of humor. He told Abigale he sounded like Wolf Man Jack.

Good days and bad days, Rick told Abigale he was afraid to go to sleep at night. He was afraid he wouldn't wake up. Abigale assured him he was being well taken care of, they were there and he didn't have to be afraid. He was having some back pain. No wonder. He had been almost constantly in bed for months. The x-rays had also showed some spots on Rick's spine that might be metastatic cancer. They also said the tumor in his chest had returned. None of that had been confirmed by biopsy. As time went on, Rick began to depend on the ventilator. He was afraid to go off of it. It was like a security blanket. During this entire ordeal, Rick's skin had stayed spotless except for all the bruises from the IV lines. Now he had a bruise on his tailbone. Supposedly, the nurses bumped it on the rails while moving him over to the cardio chair. Physical therapy started doing ultra sound treatments to the area. Rick got yet another new bed. This bed had warm sand from the waist down and it pulsated. Rick loved that bed because he was so cold most of the time.

It got harder and harder for Sam and Abigale to leave for work, especially on the days Rick was so depressed. They always prayed with him and Lucinda before they left. Lucinda had told us she read the Bible to him every night. One day Abigale wrote down a Bible verse and left it with Rick. Isaiah 41:10 "so, do not fear, for I am with you, do not be dismayed for I am your God". Abigale and Sam encouraged Lucinda to read Bible readings about healing. That particular day was bad for Rick because he knew they were planning on taking him down the next morning to try to put in a lumbar dialysis catheter due to no other places to put one. Prayer chains continued.

There is power in prayers! Rick went down for the lumbar dialysis catheter. They were able to get tunnel catheters in Rick's right subclavian vein (by his clavicle) and his right jugular (in his neck). Everyone rejoiced. Abigale knew with all the back pain Rick was already having, a catheter there would only have caused him more pain.

Abigale got a call at 2AM from Lucinda. She said Rick wanted to talk to her. He couldn't sleep and he was scared. Abigale was having problems sleeping anyway. Intuition, probably. Rick had not had a very good nurse that evening shift, but when one of the regulars came back on, they got him back on track. When he had trouble sleeping, heart rate up and fast respirations, Abigale knew it was probably infection again. The next morning, the doctor's decided to try to wean the steroids Rick was on and he couldn't tolerate it. They said he would probably have to be on them for life because one of his adrenal glands had been removed.

Tube feedings began slowly. When they tried to increase them, Rick started vomiting. Nutrition had improved some, so they didn't want to rush things now. The feedings were slowed back down. The next morning, Lucinda called to say Rick refused to get up in the cardio chair and refused to be taken off the ventilator. When Sam and Abigale got off work, they went to the hospital. Rick looked and acted great. He had been up in the chair since 12:30 that day and out on the balcony. Why was Lucinda telling them he refused? Rick just held and patted Abigale's hand and told them how much he loved and "missed all you guys".

By the next afternoon when Sam and Abigale got ready to leave again, Rick was all smiles, gave them a thumbs up and said, "I can do this'. His kidneys were doing better and dialysis was intermittently done three times a week. Wonderful news. Rehab was again being discussed, hopefully soon.

Rick had been having some trouble hearing, especially out of his right ear. Maybe due to the powerful antibiotics he had to have. One particular day, Sam told Rick that the Lord had spoke to him and told him he was going to restore Rick's hearing. Everyone had earnestly been praying for Rick to be healed head to toe. Sam ask Rick to stick his finger in his left ear. Sam turned away from Rick and ask a question. Rick answered Sam because he heard the question. Rick was so excited. The doctor's were saying if Rick could stay off the dialysis machine for 48 hours, they would take the machine out of the room. Rejoice, rejoice!

A week later, the fistula tube "fell out" again. Rick had to be sedated to replace it. It was always so obvious when Rick was over sedated. His eyes got "buggy" and his color was bad. Rick's favorite male nurse was there that day and by the end of the day, the sedation had worn off. Rick was able to get up and go out to the balcony. While he was out on the balcony, the oxygen tank ran out. His oxygen saturation dropped into the upper 80's. Once the tank was replaced, his oxygen went right back up to the upper 90's where it should be. Very optimistic in Rick's progress. He was upbeat, acting better and talking to Winnie and her boyfriend about the new baby coming. Rick was excited that if it was a boy, it was going to named after him. He wanted to be able to be in the delivery room when the baby was born.

Dear God, what next? Rick's nurse accidently broke off the hub to his dialysis catheter. Dialysis had to be stopped. There was no place to put a new line. The next day Rick went to get the catheter replaced. The radiology team was able to repair it and didn't have to try to replace it. Another prayer answered. The doctors now told Rick he had two fistulas, one large and one small in his bowel. They were still hoping they would heal on their own. All the cultures done the previous week had come back negative, but Rick was still on antibiotics due to a urinary tract infection. He was still on thyroid medication and steroids, which was going to be a life long thing. So minor after all he had been through. The doctor's again told the family that if Rick's blood pressure stayed stable, they would take out the dialysis machine and do intermittent dialysis three times a week.

Rick began to improve again. Again the doctor's were discussing moving Rick to rehab. Rick wanted to go back to his hometown rehab where he had been before but until he got stronger physically and on his feet, he may have to go somewhere else instead. Then he could be transferred to his hometown rehab. Rick was also worrying about Lucinda losing her job. Her place of employment was threatening to demote her or even fire her. She didn't want to go back to work, but what about the insurance.

The doctor's placed a wound vac on Rick's abdominal wound. In just a few days, new tissue had already started to form. Wonderful news. Rick also had finally gotten his phone back from Corella after all these months. He was able to text everyone which made it easier to keep up on his progress and know what was really happening. The family was thrilled to see in Rick's own words how he was doing and feeling.

Sam, Abigale, along with all their children, including Rick had been planning on going to the Nascar race in Daytona. Tickets and a place to stay were paid for and had been for a long time. They never dreamed that Rick would still be struggling to get well. Sam and Abigale decided not to go due to the state Rick was still in. Rick had improved and when he found out his parents were not going, he told them he wanted them to go. He told them he insisted and he wanted them to bring him a Dale Jr. hat. Very leary about going that far away, Sam and Abigale decided to go with Ariel and her husband. They kept close contact. Rick was able to get up in the chair daily. He was able to go out to the balcony and watch the 4th of July fireworks. The day after, Sam and Abigale got a phone call from Lucinda telling them Rick was having problems. She kept saying Rick was telling her, "I'm done, I'm done". His dialysis treatment had to be stopped 12 minutes early. His blood pressure dropped, pulse was running in the 140's, not breathing well and had to be put back on the ventilator. Sam and Abilgale left immediately and drove straight through the eighteen hours home from Florida. In the meantime, Carie had gone to the hospital until Sam and Abigale could get there. The doctor's had done all kinds of tests to try to find out what had happened this time. They could not find anything, but his white blood count was up to 32.2. Infection again? After the fact, Abigale found out that the feeding tube in Rick's abdomen had gotten pulled out a third time, this time with a bulb inflated on the inside. How did that happen? The surgeon was beside himself. He told Carie that he just did not know what was going on. Rick's abdomen was very painful, reddened and swollen. One of the doctor's came in to look at Rick's belly and Rick lifted his hands like he was going to karate chop him. As sick as he was, still a sense of humor. By the end of the week, Rick was in so much pain, very sedated, his eyes was rolling back in his head and the nurse just kept giving him more and more pain medication. When Abigale tried to talk to her about it, she became very upset and called the surgeon. The surgeon came in and told the family and Rick that he wasn't going to treat Rick anymore. He said he would get someone else to follow him. Hopefully, they could see what he had been missing. Everyone but Lucinda was devastated. What was happening? Sam and Abigale thought it strange the surgeon would not talk to Lucinda. He did tell them that he thought all this started at the other hospital and it needed to be stopped. Again, after the fact, Sam and Abigale found out that Lucinda had made a comment to the surgeon about this hospital being like a drive through and a dollar short. Not sure what that was all about, but it sure didn't help matters any. Lucinda had also said she had talked to the surgeon a week before and he had told her he had a brother who had been very sick and he had to make some serious decisions with his care. Abigale, at that point, decided the surgeon just didn't know what to do next with all the problems happening one right after the other. The surgeon told Abigale and Rick he didn't think he had done a very good job. Rick and Abigale both assured him they thought he had done a wonderful job. It wasn't his fault most of this was happening. They believed there was a reason for everything and things would work out. They prayed some more.

A CAT scan was done on Rick's abdomen. It showed an abscess where the drain had been pulled out the previous Saturday. Surgery was planned to drain the excess fluid that had accumulated, causing Rick pain and infection. The plan was to do wet to dry dressings on the incision to try to get it to heal.

Surgery went well. An incision was made and another drain tube inserted. Rick's blood count started to go back down to normal. Still on the ventilator, it was now discovered Rick again had two different kinds of infections in his lungs. More antibiotics. Is this ever going to end?

At that point, the Prayer Circle for Rick on the social network had grown to over 500 people, even outside the United States. That did not include all the churches, families and relatives. God is good and Rick's family believed he would bring Rick through this horrible mess somehow.

Three days after the surgeon quit treating Rick, he made a surprise visit to Rick's hospital room. He came in, ask Rick what he wanted to do. He told Rick, he would always be on pain medication and that his life would never be the same as it had previously been. He ask Rick if he wanted them to continue treatment and Rick told him that he wanted to live, with tears in his eyes. The surgeon, for some reason was under the impression that on Monday, when Rick had been so sick and was saying, "I'm done, I'm done", thought Rick wanted to die. Rick assured him that was not the case and that he didn't remember saying that because he was so sick. Rick said he actually thought he "was done", going to die. The surgeon said that was all he needed to know. More prayers answered. All prayers continued for Rick's body to be cleansed from infection and stay that way, that his kidneys and bowels would start to work normally, his fistulas to heal and get and stay off the ventialator for good. Sam and Abigale knew those were tall orders for God, but they also knew that all things are possible with God.

Four days later, the same surgeon who was back again treating Rick, came in to look at Rick's abdomen while the nurse changed the dressing. He looked, threw up his hands and walked out of the room. The drain tube was, again, not in the right place and there was some dead tissue since the last time he had seen it. The dialysis catheter had also clotted off again and that was going to have to be replaced too. Dear God, how can one person go through all this over and over and still be alive? Abigale thanked Jesus for holding her son in his arms.

Lucinda had begun again saying, "It's time to go, it's time for him to go". Amazingly, enough, Rick began to improve again after yet another surgery to remove the dead tissue in his abdomen where the abscess had been. Rick began to be more alert, watching movies, even sat up on the side of the bed for a few minutes. That was quite an improvement since he had been down for three months. Rick also told Sam he was ready to go racing. Even his mindset was improving.

Rick was still having painful daily dressing changes. He had been unconcious for so long that sometimes Abigale wondered if the staff forgot he was now awake and could realize he was having pain. They were a little too rough at times. Lucinda evidently also forgot. She told Abigale about watching a dressing change at one point and the doctor sticking his hand in Rick's belly? Lucinda said it "was cool". It really was painful for Rick. Abigale apologized to Rick and told him that she thought they just were not thinking and not used to having him awake. After being in bed for so long, Rick began to complain of his neck hurting. Abigale made him a Dale Jr. neck pillow. It did help, but it wasn't long the pillow disappeared. Over the next few days, Rick continued to improve. He was again doing trach trials, watching scary movies on TV, getting up in the chair, going out to the balcony, urine output was picking up and he was more like himself than he had been in months.

Sam and Abigale had again returned home to work. A few nights later Rick was having trouble sleeping. This made his parents nervous because that was always one of the signs of trouble lurking around the corner. Rick's white blood count was up slightly. He was confused, talking out of his head, picking at things in the air and talking to people that weren't there. Abigale had never seen him this way. She suspected medication as the culprit. Lucinda assured her it was not more medication. Abigale and Sam returned to the hospital. They found out the night nurse had given Rick a "sleeping cocktail". Abigale was furious. The "sleeping cocktail" consisted of 50mg of Haldol, 2 mg of Ativan and 12.5 of Benadryl. What in the world were they thinking? Besides all that, the tech who came in to do the ultrasound on the bruised area on his bottom, kept pushing the pain button for him (a big no no). Rick's pulse was once again running in the 120's and blood pressure was very low. His heart rate at one point had dropped to 0 and they had to give him Atropine. Medications sure done a number on him and everyone knew it, including Lucinda.

By the end of the month, Rick still had two infections in his lungs, filling up with fluid, still on dialysis three times a week, and back on the ventilator while taking dialysis. At times, Rick was talking around the ventilator and it would pop off when he would talk. Rick was still having good days and bad days. He wanted to go home and he missed everyone and his puppies. Sam and Abigale tried hard to keep his spirits up, but it was so hard for Rick.

The doctor's started talking about transferring Rick to rehab an hour from his home. Slow improvement again, still on the ventilator, changed the trach to a smaller one in order to be one step closer to removing it, still had the wound vac to try to heal the fistulas, but still having a lot of drainage from it. The wound care nurses said Rick's belly was healing slower than they wanted, but it was healing. More answered prayers. Rick's mood was better and he put orders in for A & W Root Beer and Dasani water. Sam and Abigale were delighted to give him anything he wanted as long as the doctor's said it was okay.

Lucinda's work had told her she needed to be back to work by October or she was without a job. That meant no insurance. Rick could not go without insurance. He had come this far.

The last day of the month, Rick was taken off the ventilator and transferred to rehab an hour from where he lived. It would be easier for family to visit. So much closer to home and so much better for Rick, mentally.

Rick once again was transferred by ambulance to rehab an hour from his home. That day started out to be very disturbing for Abigale and it should have been a happy day. First thing that morning, even with the joy that God had answered yet another prayer and Rick was one step closer to home, Abigale started getting messages from Lucinda's friend, the nurse. She was saying all kinds of insulting things about Abigale not knowing what she was doing as a nurse, mainly because since graduating college, Abigale had not furthered her education. Abigale was pretty sure she knew where all that came from. This went on most of the day until Sam and Abigale followed the ambulance to the rehab to meet Rick. A lot of what the friend was saying had to come from Lucinda. Otherwise, she would not have known any of it. Abigale knew who was behind this escapade. Abigale finally told the friend she needed mental help, left it at that and blocked her from her social network. Nothing was going to spoil Sam and Abigale's joy and encouragement of Rick being one step closer to home.

Sam and Abigale joked later about the way Sam followed the ambulance. He ran two red lights and he was speeding. That was very unusual for Sam. He never drives like that and Rick got a kick out of it all. Rick would wave at us while we were stopped at a stop light from the back of the ambulance. Sam and Abigale wanted Rick to know they were still there. Lucinda rode in the front seat of the ambulance.

When Rick finally got to rehab, after the staff got him settled in, Rick was downright mad. When Lucinda wasn't happy, neither was Rick. The staff wouldn't let Lucinda stay in the room, take her laptop in or use her cell phone. It was a relief to the family as that should have happened months ago due to all the sources of infections in the past. Sam and Abigale prayed this would be the beginning of a well deserved recovery for Rick. Once Rick talked to Sam and Abigale and they explained the reasoning for not letting Lucinda bring all that in the room, he started apologizing and said, "I lost my head". Good Lord, Rick had every right for these moods. As the days went on, Rick became more comfortable at rehab. They still had not got to do much with him physically, but they had told Sam and Abigale they didn't think Rick even needed dialysis any longer. They were working on increasing his protein in his IV nutrition to help with healing and skin care. Plans for a diet to help him get enough protein and calories then eventually Rick would be able to get rid of the IV nutrition. Abigale was so encouraged and loved their way of thinking. Rick was actually the point of interest, finally.

Lucinda eventually got a room down the hall fixed up for her. She was still not happy about the arrangements, but rehab had a family meeting and it was so encouraging. The drainage from Rick's abdomen had lessened, it seemed, but he was still on antibiotics for lung infections. Before the first week was over,

Lucinda had managed to have her cell phone and lap top back in Rick's room.

The first week of August, rehab decided that Rick did need dialysis. Due to his infections and antibiotics, his kidney function numbers were increasing and he was filling up with fluid once again. Physical therapy and occupational therapy were working with Rick daily. Rick's family was hoping that would help him gain strength.

Rehab had talked with the surgeon from the hospital Rick had been at. He had told them they could try Rick on some soft, ground food. They brought Rick some mashed potatoes, three chopped up french fries, one chopped up chicken tender and some chocolate milk. Abigale fed Rick because he was still very weak. She told him to open wide when he was ready and she would shovel it in. Rick ate well. The nurse made the comment that Abigale was a miracle worker. Everyone had been so helpless through the entire ordeal, Abigale was delighted to help in any way she could. After Rick got finished eating, Abigale heard a gurgling noise. She looked down and Rick had mashed potatoes coming out his side where the fistula was. Abigale didn't want to worry Rick so she put a napkin down to absorb the food. Lucinda noticed what Abigale did and said, "It's coming out, isn't it?" Rick had an awful look on his face. Abigale felt so bad for Rick.

Evening came and Rick told Abigale he was going to take a nap. He told her when his supper came to wake him up so he could eat. Lucinda didn't wake him up until 9PM that evening when Winnie and her boyfriend came to visit. She said she wanted to wait until they got there. Abigale let everyone know on her social network about Rick eating. Her phone went off all night with messages from so many people so happy for Rick. So many people praying. Rick, by now, was a household name.

Rehab put Rick in isolation because he had infection in his blood now. Abigale just couldn't understand why so many infections all the time. He would seem to get better and down he would go again. He also had the same infection in his lungs he had at the hospital. Rehab said it was very contageous. Isolation finally managed like it should have been months ago.

A minister came to visit Rick while he was at rehab. The minister was from another church. He talked with Rick about baptism. He told Rick that if he wasn't baptized under a certain scripture, he was going to hell. Sam and Abigale was furious. How could someone do such a thing, especially with someone so sick and vulnerable.

Finally, after all the months of Sam and Abigale trying to get Lucinda to go home, she finally did. That day, all Rick would say was, "I feel awful, I feel terrible". Later, Sam and Lucinda found out that Rick had been put on a continuous dose of Dilaudid again. They discussed this with the staff and that was taken off. Rick soon began to feel better.

Rick's phone went off and he was sleeping. Abigale picked it up to answer. Rick opened his eyes and shook his head no. Abigale said, "You don't want me looking at it?" Rick shook his head no. Abigale laid the phone down, but she had already seen several messages where Lucinda had talked about shopping trips. Abigale had suspected she was lying about not leaving Rick's side. That's what she told everyone. By the end of the day, Rick was feeling better. Abigale helped him eat 7 bites of cheeseburger and 6 bites of mashed potates and gravy. Sam, Abigale and their family were making plans for Rick's Praise The Lord Party when he got well and home. They had so much to celebrate and make up for.

Not too long after Rick was at rehab, Sam and Abigale found out that Lucinda had been getting money from Sam's family. She had been getting money from his cousins and some of his aunts and uncles. She was even telling them she needed more. Sam was furious. They knew of the thousands of dollars she had made off of Rick's illness, not to mention the disability check he was still receiving every month, Winnie working two jobs, Winnie's boyfriend's job and no house payment which was in review for non-payment. At the same time, Lucinda's ex-husband was helping remodel a bathroom at Lucinda's house into a nursery. How embarrassing and how dare her to pump Sam's family for money. She was making quite a living off this horrible ordeal.

The second week of August, Rick's appetite had decreased. He had filled up with fluid and his blood pressure had dropped. He had to be transferred from rehab to a hospital nearby for continuous dialysis. When he first got to the hospital, they said they couldn't use his dialysis catheter and it would have to be replaced. That was a worry, especially with all the blood clots and very few places to put one.

Abigale and Carie went to the hospital after getting off work. They waited for Rick to get finished in radiology. They were able to get in two new lines. One for dialysis and one for all the IV medications. When Rick came out, he was jerking his head all around, telling Carie and Abigale he loved them. Abigale again told Rick she would trade places with him in a heartbeat if she could. He shook his head "NO". By the time Carie and Abigale left, the staff was priming the dialysis machine to start dialysis and to give Rick some blood. On their way home, Lucinda called to tell them that the dialysis access had already clotted off. Dear God!! They said they could not give him heparin because he was allergic to it. Where did that come from? He was not allergic to it, just sensitive to medicines of any kind if he gets too much. The doctor said Rick's platelets were very low and they were worried about heparin induced thrombocytopenia. Sometimes, blood thinners like heparin can affect the bone marrow from making platelets. Rick's platelets were low and could cause excessive bleeding. He also had that complication many times before. With the dialysis catheter being clotted, dialysis was again on hold. Abigale didn't know how all this was going to turn out, and turned it once again over to the Lord. She also prayed to God and gave Rick back to him as she had done years ago when Rick had Hodgkins. Abigale told the Lord, "Your will be done". Rick was wanting to talk to the doctors to see if he was going to have to keep going through this over and over again. He did still say he wanted to live. He had such determination and fight.

When Abigale would return to work, everyone was always interested in what what happening with Rick. One of her co-workers ask her one day, "Are you sure there's not some Munchausen going on here?" Abigale knew something wasn't right, but Munchausen never entered her mind. She had learned about Munchausen by Proxy in nursing school, but it was so rare except in mothers and children.

During the night, Rick had told the nurse he didn't want any more pain medication. When the day nurse arrived, he was in terrible pain and she medicated him. He rested some. They decided to try to put something called TPA in his dialysis catheter to try to declot it. Amazingly, it worked and his dialysis was once again going. Rick's family sent messages and prayer requests out. They got messages from their kids saying pray, pray, pray. By the end of the day, the hospital staff was able to get Rick off one of the blood pressure medicines, his blood pressure was good and he was asking for something to drink.

On the fourth day after Rick had been admitted to the hospital, one of the nurses came to the door and ask Abigale if she could talk to her. Abigale had already decided to not say anything to anyone of the suspicions they had about Lucinda because no one listened anyway. The nurse took Abigale out to the hallway and started asking her questions about how long Rick and Lucinda had been married, how long they had known each other and finally Abigale got the direction the nurse was heading. Abigale told her, "Look, I have tried to tell people for months about her and no one would listen, I'm not going there now." The nurse looked at Abigale and said, "Munchausen". Abigale was in shock. After all this time of trying to tell people, finally someone had noticed. Abigale told her this and by that time was crying hysterically, and the nurse said, "I noticed it the first day".

The next day, one of Rick's doctor's came in and was questioning Sam and Abigale about Rick's living will. Abigale told him his living will stated he wanted everything done possible unless he was declared brain dead. The doctor said, "I know, but things have changed". Abigale told him to go in and talk to Rick himself. The doctor said he would tomorrow. Abigale told him he needed to do it right then and there. He did go talk with Rick and Rick told him he wanted everything done possible to keep him alive.

Out in the hallway, the discussion continued. Abigale ask the doctor if he had talked to the nurse who Abigale had talked to the day before. He said, "No". He took Sam and Abigale into a private room and they talked. After a while, the doctor said, "It's all making sense now. That line should not have clotted off so soon". They also talked about Lucinda's friend, the nurse. Her last name was never mentioned, but the doctor knew exactly who they were talking about. He said, "It all makes sense now, she is no longer working here". Sam and Abigale went to talk to the nurse manager. She moved Rick across from the nurse's station where he could be watched closer. They used the excuse that they needed that dialysis machine for another patient. Lucinda was not happy. She knew the staff was watching her. Rick also was not happy because when Lucinda wasn't happy, she made that reflect on Rick.

One evening the next week, Lucinda and Abigale talked on the phone at 6:30 PM and Abigale was encouraged because she said Rick got liquids for supper. Rick didn't want any of the liquids so the nurse made him some flavored ice. Lucinda said she fed it to him. An alarm went off in Abigale's head. She felt very uneasy. She ask Lucinda if the nurse fed it to him or if Lucinda fed it to him. She said she did and he did fine. Abigale ask if he was coughing or anything and she said no. I have seen her feed him and she does it very fast. She didn't give him time to swallow. About 10:30 PM that same evening, Lucinda called again. She told Abigale she forgot to tell her something. The hospital staff thought Rick had aspirated after he ate the flavored ice. Abigale's heart fell. She knew something was up. The staff had to put him back on the ventilator. They began to talk of maybe transferring Rick back to the hospital where he had his last surgery. Abigale ask them what they were able to do for him there that this hospital couldn't do. If not anything, Rick could not handle another transfer.

The dialysis catheter was clotted again by the middle of the month. Rick was not happy. He said the nurses were mean to him and they were rough with him when Sam and Abigale were not around. He was in a lot of pain, even his skin hurt. A nurse put up a sign in his room that said, "Move gently, skin very sore". Thankfully, they were able to replace his dialysis catheter in his neck this time. How long will he have to deal with this?

Two days later, Abigale got a phone call from Lucinda's aunt from out of state. She had been in town visiting and had went to see Rick. She said that Rick wanted her to call Abigale and let her know he wanted to talk to her. Abigale went to talk to him. He cried a lot, told Abigale he thought everyone was giving up on him and he was lonely. He also told Abigale that people were talking to him about dying. Abigale ask who and he wouldn't say. Abigale ask Lucinda and she said her and her mother were discussing it with the palliative care nurse in the room but Rick was asleep. Obviously not!!! Abigale was upset. She ask them not to be discussing that in the room anymore. On the day Rick was admitted to rehab, Abigale had noticed some flyers in the waiting room about palliative care. It crossed her mind that if Lucinda picked up on that, she would be calling them. Abigale cringed. Evidently, that was what happened.

Rick's family decided to have a card shower for him to try to cheer him up. He got many, many cards. It did help some, but he was having trouble seeing and couldn't read the cards. Ariel came and brought Rick some black reading glasses, a bible and a magazine. It thrilled him to pieces. You would have thought that he had a million bucks. He didn't let them out of his sight. When Rick's family would leave and return, Rick's glasses would be lying on a table behind him where he couldn't see or reach them. He would ask for them and his cards so he could look at them.

Abigale thanked God for all the people who sent them and cherish that happiness they brought to him.

The hospital was still working on better nutrition, his wound was staying dryer, labs were not bad and dialysis was going well.

A few days later, a doctor who came to Abigale's hospital once a week made rounds to see Rick. He had no idea they were related. He printed off the information for Abigale of all of the four different infections that Rick had in his abdominal wound. At that time, he said there was none in his blood. Rick was on five different antibiotics. The doctor just kept saying he was sorry. Rick was having dark red drainage coming out of his drains. The doctors decided to do another CAT scan. Two of Abigale's sisters and one of her brothers came to visit while Sam and Abigale went to their grandson's birthday party. As soon as they got to the party, one of Abigale's sisters called to say there were big blood clots coming from the drains and Rick's blood pressure was very low. Sam and Abigale went right back to the hospital. By the time they arrived, Rick was some better. His blood pressure was better, he had gotten some fluid, some blood and the bleeding had slowed down. The doctor had told us the CAT scan had shown, once again, the lesions on Rick's spine. Lucinda was acting all concerned. Abigale reminded her that they had already been told that a long time ago and that it was not a concern at that time. The infections were a more concerning issue. The doctor agreed.

In the midst of all this mess, Lucinda decided she was going to start nursing school. Sam and Abigale stayed with Rick while she went to register. When she returned, she brought her mother back with her. They walked right into the room with their purse, backpacks and books. Sam and Ariel was furious. They went to the nurse manager again. The nurses had told Ariel that if she took the glasses and Bible into Rick's room, they would have to stay in there due to the isolation. Now here, Lucinda and her mother were carrying things in and out and not a word was said. The nurse manager stopped that right quick. Abigale knew nurses get busy and sometimes don't pay attention.

The next Monday Abigale got a call from Lucinda telling her that Rick had gotten confused and pulled out his central line. She kept saying, "What does this mean?" She just kept repeating that phrase. She proceeded to tell Abigale how she wasn't supposed to be back in Rick's room at the change of shifts, but the nurses were all sitting around talking and laughing, catching up on their weekend and not paying any attention to her being there. After all these months and all Rick had been through, he had never even attempted to bother any of his tubes or lines. The doctor's put him on Ativan again and he slept the entire day. Rick's doctor had called Abigale that same day. He was upset with the nursing staff. He said they had been talking to Rick about dying and that he had trouble with that kind of thing before. He assured Abigale it wouldn't happen again. He also said he was glad the line was out because he was afraid it was getting infected. There was still one line available that could be used.

Over the next couple days, it was more of the same. Ups and downs. Rick being very sleepy. The doctor finally backed down on the Ativan and Rick became more alert. The ventilator settings were turned down three times after that. This hospital was a religious hospital. Above the door in Rick's room was a statue of Jesus on the cross. When things got rough for Rick, his family would point to the statue and tell Rick to keep his eyes on the cross. The family talked a lot with Rick about Jesus and what he had been through so that we all might live forever. They even talked about the movie, Passion of the Christ and what all Jesus went through for us all. Rick improved again, swabbing out his own mouth, throwing the swabs at the waste basket and shooting rubber bands at the nurses. He was one amazing man.

Then Rick began filling up with fluid again and they couldn't do his dialysis because his blood pressure was too low. All of the bleeding he had, had stopped completely. Carie and Abigale were visiting one evening after work and Lucinda seemed very nervous. She continually paced around in the room, studying the machines, studying the dialysis machine. They recognized her nervous habits by now. She was standing with her feet apart, cross her arms and twist back and forth at the waist. She was doing this then and studying the dialysis machine very hard. Abigale told Carie, "Don't be surprised if something dont't happen to the dialysis machine". The next morning Lucinda called to tell Abigale the dialysis machine stopped working due to overpressure. Abigale kept remembering the song, "One Day At A Time, Dear Jesus". That's the way it had been for almost a year. Since the dialysis machine wasn't working and the heparin had to be stopped, the dialysis catheter was also not working. Rick had to go down for yet another new line. That was put off a couple days due to an emergency with another patient, therefore Rick's kidney function labs doubled. On the last day of the month, they were able to get in the needed line and dialysis was restarted late that night.

The next morning Sam and Abigale went back to the hospital. They were waiting in the waiting room when Abigale's phone rang. It was the doctor telling her he needed to talk to her. Abigale told him they were in the waiting room and had been for over an hour. He wanted to tell them that Rick's blood pressure dropped really low and they were having a hard time keeping it up. The longer they were there, the better Rick got. The hemetologist came to tell them they had examined Rick's blood under a microscope and there were no signs of leukemia, lymphoma or cancer. Rick seemed to be very angry with Abigale for some reason that day. Something he was trying to tell her about Lucinda. He was so in and out of it, they couldn't quite make out what he was trying to say. He would look at Lucinda as if he was asking her permission to answer us. He became more alert that day and started to complain of his neck being sore. Abigale told him it was probably where he had pulled that line out. Rick said, "What line, when did that happen?" Abigale said, "That line you pulled out of your neck". Rick replied, "I didn't pull it out". Abigale looked at Sam and ask Rick, "Who pulled it out Rick. Did the nurse accidently pull it out?" "No" he replied. Abigale kept questioning him and Rick finally said, "Whoever was in the room". Abigale's heart sank. That was finally the closest to the truth they had been since the beginning. Sam and Abigale again had a talk with the nurse manager.

The next evening, right before midnight, Abigale got another call from Lucinda saying Rick wanted to talk to her. Abigale ask about what and she said Rick was saying he wanted to die. She kept saying broken words like she was standing in front of him reading his lips and he was telling her, "I . . . want . . . to . . . talk . . . to . . . you . . . I . . . want . . . you . . . here . . . now". Abigale called the nurse on duty and the nurse said Rick was resting fine. Abigale called Lucinda back and told her what the nurse had said. Abigale told Lucinda it was late, that she and Carie were coming the next morning. Abigale could not stand to not go. Her and Carie left for the hospital. When they arrived, Lucinda and her mother were asleep on the couches in the waiting room. Abigale and Carie went back to see Rick. He also was asleep. They sat there for over an hour. Rick woke up and ask what they were doing there at that time. The nurse told Abigale she had not heard Rick ask for her. Rick told Abigale, "I can't do this anymore. Please let me go. Please let me die" Abigale began to cry and told Rick, "Please don't talk like that. I am not God and I don't decide how long you will live or when you will die". Abigale and Carie stayed with Rick until he went back to sleep and then returned to the waiting room. Lucinda and her mother were still asleep and Abigale pecked Lucinda on the shoulder several times to wake her up. When she finally woke up, Abigale said, "I guess he got settled down?" She said, "Yes, we stayed with him until about 12:30". Abigale told Lucinda what Rick had said and also told her that it was not going to happen. They knew Lucinda and Corella had been discussing dying with Rick and the staff. At 6:30 the next morning, Abigale was up and ready to go back to see Rick when visitors were allowed back in his room. The nurse came to the waiting room and told Lucinda that Rick was asking for her. Lucinda came back to the waiting room and told Abigale that Rick was trying to pull out his trach and a respiratory therapists was in the room with him. Abigale and Carie went to Rick's room. He was sleeping and there was no one else in the room. When Rick woke up, he saw Abigale and Carie and started talking about wanting to die again. One of the palliative care nurses just happen to come to the room and ask to speak with Abigale and Carie. They told the nurse that they were not going to let Rick die. The nurse said she was going to get a psych consult and if Rick passed it, they would take everything off and let Rick die. Abigale called a friend of hers at the hospital where she worked. The friend told Abigale they could get a court order to stop this madness. When the doctor came in, he told them he was going to carry on treatment as planned. There would be no psych consult. He was not happy. Corella finally awoke that morning and ask how Rick was doing. Abigale was very angry and told her "not good". She also told Corella that they knew her and Lucinda had been talking to Rick about dying, it was not going to happen and they needed to quit talking to him about it. Corella told Abigale, "If you really loved your son, you would have been here 24/7". Abigale was so upset and angry. It was not true. What right did she have to judge Abigale? She had thought so many times about having the state police stop Corella enroute to the hospital and check her bags. The family believed she was bringing Lucinda medication to give Rick. Later on, after Carie had heard about the conversation between Abigale and Corella, Carie let Corella have it and gave her a piece of her mind. Corella deserved it. She was so oblivious to how much love our family had for each other. Sam and Abigale talked with Rick about us staying continuously with him. He wanted that and Lucinda, all of a sudden, had no objections to the plans. All of a sudden, she didn't want to be there after months of Rick's family trying to get her to leave. Abigale believed Lucinda knew her job was done. Sam stayed with Rick that night. Plans were for Abigale to work the next day and stay with Rick the weekend. Rick's vital signs were better than they had been in a long time.

Rick awoke the next morning telling Sam he wanted to die. Sam called Abigale at work and told her to come to the hospital. He told Abigale that Rick was talking about wanting to die again. Abigale was so upset. Her nurse manager tried to talk to her. Abigale told her, "I can't let him die!" She said, "Abigale if that is what he really wants and he has been through so much". Abigale felt she had been selfish. She didn't want to lose her son. Abigale called all the kids and they all left for the hospital. On the way, Abigale called Lucinda to tell her what was happening. Lucinda had returned home the night before. Abigale told her, "If that is what he really wants, then I have to abide by his wishes". Lucinda said, "Okay, we will come but I won't stay tonight and interfere with your time with him". Abigale said, "Lucinda, do you not understand? Rick is probably going to die today". Rick's family arrived and Rick was very angry, pounding his hands on the bed and crying "Please let me die". The family took turns staying at his bedside. One minute he was swatting at them and the next minute he would pull down Abigale's isolation mask and say "I love you". They believed he couldn't tell who was there. He couldn't see well and he couldn't hear well by that time. Dale ask Abigale to please do something. He said, "Mom, he is suffering". Four hours later, Lucinda, her mother, Rick's minister, Winnie and her boyfriend finally arrived. Abigale told the nurses she was going to abide by Rick's wishes. The plan was to take everything off and let Rick die as he wished. The staff ask if the family wanted to be present when they removed all the life saving equipment. Everyone but Abigale was there. She just couldn't stand to watch. Maybe that was being selfish too.

That afternoon the nurses removed all the life saving equipment attached to Rick, gave Rick medication to relax him. They moved him to a "comfort" room. Sam's youngest sister and her husband came to be with the family. Rick's minister also stayed and at one point, Sam and Abigale spilled all their suspicions to him. He really didn't believe it, but he had not seen or been there the entire time and he for sure did not know the real Lucinda. It's hard to believe that there are people out there that want to hurt other people for their gain, but the truth is, there are. Sadly, but true.

A few hours passed. Everyone was at Rick's bedside. Lucinda sat by the head of the bed with one hand on his head and texting on her phone with the other hand. Abigale figured she was getting more advice from her nurse friend. Sure enough, the nurses took Abigale aside out in the hallway. They said they wanted to explain why they were not going to give Rick a bath at this time. Abigale assured them she already knew the reason. Lucinda had ask for them to give Rick a bath. Most healthcare workers, in most instances, know the more you move someone who is dying around, the quicker you could cause them to die. Abigale was not surprised at this request. Just another tip from Lucinda's nurse friend.

Rick looked so peaceful for the first time in months. At one point, he was even smiling the old natural smile he used to have. Was the time near? Was he seeing God or relatives who had gone before him? Was he seeing the heavenly Angels?

Lucinda left the room and Abigale sat down by Rick's bed, held his hand and rubbed his forehead. She whispered in his ear, "It's okay if you want to go Rick. We love you and everyone is here with you". It was getting close to midnight. Rick's minister had been there most of the day. He was getting tired and couldn't get comfortable. Lucinda returned to the room. Rick's minister said, "I'm going to have to go, but I want to pray with you all first". He said a wonderful prayer, saying Rick was healed two years ago when he was saved. That was so true. As soon as the minister said "Amen" Rick took his last breath. Abigale said, "I believe he is gone". The minister said, "I guess he didn't want me to leave". Rick knew too, he didn't want him to leave before he passed away. He loved him so much.

Abigale and the family waited for the nurses to come in and pronounce Rick, but they didn't come in until well after midnight. The family knew they would have questions about where to send Rick's body and about funeral arrangements. To the family's surprise, the arrangements had already been made. Abigale told the nursing staff that she wanted an autopsy done. She wanted to know what all Rick had in his system. Lucinda was standing there and said, "you want the hospital to do it?". The nurse also ask, "You want the hospital or coroner to do the autopsy?" Again, Abigale did not know that if a hospital done an autopsy, the blood was not checked, only if a county coroner had done the autopsy. Obviously, Lucinda did. The nurse friend had really helped her with her homework. The family found that out a few weeks later when they picked up the autopsy.

Sam and Abigale had evidently fallen back to sleep in each others arms. They were awakened by the phone ringing. She jumped to her feet like she was shot out of cannon. She was so used to being startled by the phone ringing. She will always shake inside with a certain ring tone on her phone. It was one of Abigale's sisters. Her entire family and Sam's sister and her husband were coming, bringing food and to help them out those next few days. The following days were a blur. They had a wonderful family, co-workers and so many friends. They were all there the next few days helping us through until the funeral. They weren't afraid to talk about Rick and what a funny, strong, wonderful, brave man he had been.

Lucinda had put the obituary in the paper, not mentioning any of Rick's siblings, nieces or nephews. Rick loved them all so much. She did mention her unborn grandchild, Winnie and her boyfriend. Abigale ask her to relist it with the information Rick would like to have had. She did and it was much more tasteful.

It was a very nice funeral. Rick had his favorite shirts hanging above his casket. Nascar, his favorite baseball team and hunting. His casket had an embroidered deer on the top. Abigale's brother-in-law, who also is a minister, spoke along with Rick's minister. Boyd spoke of the fun loving person Rick had been, the jokes and the pranks he used to pull. Lucinda had made a movie running during the funeral with pictures of the old days, their friends drinking and partying. Abigale thought it an insult to Rick because he had no longer been that person. She didn't say anything, but Rick's minister noticed. He spoke of not knowing that man in those pictures. He had a talk with Lucinda the night of the showing and some of the pictures were taken off the screen. He said he knew Rick as a saved Christian and again said that Rick was healed two years ago when he was saved. He also said that Rick, as sick as he had been, told the minister that he prayed for him everyday. That made Sam and Abigale proud to know that they had such a strong son with a strong faith. Rick loved to hear his minister's daughter sing and play the guitar. She sang at the funeral and it was beautiful. Abigale had told Lucinda she would like for the minister's daughter to sing Rise Again by Dallas Holmes. The minister called the day before the funeral and said they couldn't find the music or words. Come to find out, Lucinda had told them the wrong title and artist. It was too late by then. A friend of Abigale's came to the showing. She is also a well known soloist. She was asking who was going to sing. Abigale was telling her about the song she had requested. Her friend went to the Bible Book store and had them make a CD of the song. It was played and made the funeral complete.

So many family and friends came. A lot of Rick's friends came. One mentioned that cancer was a bad thing. Abigale had to let him know that Rick did not pass away with cancer as Lucinda had been telling everyone. The autopsy said he passed away with septic shock, severe infection.

Another close friend of Abigale's gave her a picture entitled "The Broken Chain" . . . We little knew that morning that God would call your name, In life we loved you dearly, In death we do the same. It broke our hearts to lose you, you did not go alone, for part of us went with you, the day God called you home. You left us peaceful memories, your love is still our guide; and though we cannot see you, you are always at our side. Our family chain is broken and nothing seems the same, but as God calls us one by one the chain will link again . . . Abigale's co-workers had also given her some beautiful wind chimes. They hang on the front porch and remind Abigale daily of the love she had for Rick. They will all reunite some glorious day.

A few weeks after Rick's death, Ariel and Abigale went to get Rick's autopsy. Rick died from septic shock. There was nothing on the report about what was in his blood stream. Abigale ask about that and the hospital coroner said that if the autopsy had been done by a county coroner it would have been checked. The autopsy talked about Rick's infections, he had many tumors everywhere, the lesions on his bones and areas of suspected metastatic cancer. None of the cancer was ever biopsied or confirmed. The pathologist also said that if he had known of any suspicious activity, it would have automatically went to the county coroner. The staff did know, but it doesn't matter now.

Rick's family have had people tell them, "It was God's plan". No, God doesn't do things like that. He doesn't make people suffer or go through torture. The devil does. It was God's plan to take Rick when he could no longer fight. People have also said, "Let the dead rest in peace". He is resting in peace, finally, but he will never be forgotten or will we ever forget he lived and had such an impact on so many lives.

Rick's siblings wanted some of Rick's belongings, especially all they had bought for him. They had a hard time getting them. Dale wanted the deer he missed that time and Rick got him the following weekend. He ended up getting all four of Rick's deer heads and Dale shared them with the other siblings. They got a trunk full of stuff, mainly junk, but in the bottom Abigale found notes and cards Rick had kept from when he had Hodgkins. People had sent him cards and notes of encouragement. One of his cousins had also had cancer years ago before Rick and those notes and cards were in the bottom of the trunk So many special memories and they meant so much to him. He kept them all those years.

As for Lucinda, there is no communication. Rick's family prays for her and has forgiven her, but will never forget what has happened. Lucinda and Rick knew each other less than nine years and he was gone. She was getting on with her life a little over a month after Rick's death. She had pictures of her and her drinking buddies plastered all over a social network. She arrived in ER Christmas eve with another man after a sledding accident. She had new braces on her teeth less than six weeks after he was gone. She is spending money like it is water. Not for Rick's family to worry about. Rick is at peace and God will deal with the rest. They are not the judge nor the jury.

Abigale's biggest regret was that she hadn't quit work to stay with Rick constantly. She knows in her heart that it would have been impossible to have prevented most of what happened. Still praying for strength, Rick's family tries to live the way God wants them to live so they can all meet again someday.

Many things have happened to let the family know Rick is alright and in a better place. Abigale always sits a few moments in her car after work to gather her thoughts after a busy day. The clouds had looked different one particular day. As she was sitting there, she looked up and there right before her was a perfect praying angel with Rick's perfect signature underneath. She groped for her camera to take a picture, not realizing she had forgotten it at home that morning. Some people thinks she's crazy, but it was there. She has seen the words LOVE spelled out in the clouds, a green cup that rocked continuously in her kitchen until that day she saw the angel. Rick will be forever showing his family signs that he is near. His siblings have had their TV channels turn off and on with no explanation. Maybe one, coincidence, but all three, no.

<u>Carie wrote this one week after Rick's death</u>

It's already been a week today since you've been gone
It already feels like it's been so long
I miss your smile, your laugh and your joking ways
Man, those were the good ole days
You brought joy and laughter to all of us
We will miss you so, so much
You were very sick for so long
Now you're in Heaven listening to the Angels sing you a beautiful song
We all wanted so much for you to get well
I'm sorry you went through so much hell
Keep your eyes on Jesus, Rick, he will heal you, that's what we would say
And he did in his own way
Say good-bye to all the pain and suffering you've endured
Now you are forever cured
I went to your grave this morning just to talk and visit
I wished so much I could hear your voice
But I know that's not a choice
I knelt down over you in the rain
My head in my hands with tears running down my face
I'm sure you saw my pain
I know you would not want me to be sad
But this hurt I feel is like no other
After all, I have just lost my big brother
No matter how hard it was to say good-bye
I am very thankful I got that chance
Standing there by your side, I told I love you, will miss you
And you took once last glance
Life will never be the same without you here
But I believe you will always be near
I'll be looking forward to seeing you again
So I will always be sure to pray and say Amen
There are so many things I will miss about you
But I'm gonna try to stay strong
That's what you would tell me to do
Oh what a beautiful impression on my life you have made
I will miss you and never forget you Ricky Lane

Abigale sent thank you notes to special people after the funeral. Everyone had been so kind and helped them out so much. She also sent notes to the last hospital Rick had been in and to let them know he didn't survive. She sent one to the last surgeon too thanking him for "fixing" Rick and letting him taste food after so many months. Sam, Abigale and their family received this note from the surgeon close to Christmas that first year. It meant so much to them and touched their hearts.

My thoughts and prayers are with you during this holiday season after Rick's death. His courage and love for his family remain with me to this day as an example for how I should live my life. Rick taught me a great deal that I will never forget and I believe that is the definition of a life well-lived, even so disappointingly short

<u>A co-worker of Sam's wrote this and gave it to him:</u>

Do not stand at my grave and weep
I am not here
I do not sleep
I am a thousand winds that blow
I am the diamond glints of snow
I am the sunlight on ripened grain
I am the gentle autumn rain
Do not stand at my grave and cry
I am not here, I did not die

The first year anniversary of Rick's death, his family met at the graveyard to put new flowers on Rick's headstone along with a solar cross. Carie wrote this message to read . . .
It's so hard to believe that you have already been gone a year
There's not a day that's went by that we haven't thought of you and not one day that we haven't shed a tear
Life over this past year had definitely been so different, none of us are the same
Family get together's and holidays are hard, cause we miss you and really wish you could have came

We all still try to make the best out of the time we have together, we
reminisce a lot about the days when you were here and the times we
had
You not being there like you used to be, makes us all so sad
We all speak of you often, we love to talk about all the funny things
you done
And how you were always so much fun
We hold on to everything about you, how you looked, the way your
voice sounded, things that we have that were yours, things that you
have said
All these things stick in our head
Remembering you is the way our days start
The spirit of you Rick, we will forever hold tightly in our hearts. We
all have so many memories of you that we will forever cherish
And no matter how many years go by our memories and love for you
will never perish
You are the first thing we think about when we wake up everyday,
and the last at night when we lay down in bed
We think of you and wish there was something else we could have
done or said
But we have all come to realize that God needed you more and even
though we know you are in a better place
Our hearts still ache, and would give the world to see your face
It's only been one year since you've been gone, and as long as we are
hear on earth and you are in heaven
We will miss you and think of you everyday, even when it's been
year thirty-seven
We will always believe that you're always around us
Messages in the clouds and on clear, nice days when the wind picks
up and blows
These are the things that sends chills from our head to our toes
When that cool feeling hits our skin out of the blue
It makes us smile cause we know it is you
You come to us in body, through our dreams is the only way that can be
And you also like to play tricks on some of us while we are watching
TV
Some people may say
Why do you hang on to Rick this way

Torturing yourself leaves you nothing to gain
Constantly talking about him and holding on just causes more pain
But some people don't understand that holding on does help to heal
And I wouldn't expect them to know how we feel
Talking about him helps us not to ever forget and makes us stronger
And the days between melt down's are getting a little longer
Rick was so many things to all of us, a son, a brother, an uncle and so much more
A true fighter down to the core
God took you home on the day last year, 2010
And we will all be ecstatic to see you again
Death for all of us is now not so scary
Of course we hope to live full lives and be merry
Now it just leaves us with something to look forward to
And that's living eternal life with you
So until each of us are called to walk through the pearly gate
We will keep our faith and not hate
God will handle the things that are on our mind
And justice he will find
Turning this poem from sad to funny is what I want to try
Cause we know you would want us to laugh instead of always cry
It is very comforting knowing where you are and that you are safe in the kingdom of of the Lord
We can just see you now, roaming around looking for a trick to play on Grandma cause you are bored
We hope you are getting to do all the fishing that you want up there, sitting back and relaxing without a care
As the years go by we will each start to join you, maybe by then you will have grown some hair
So until we meet again when we have our mopey days and depressed is how we are feeling
We will just think of how you would have laughed at mom's story about dad's leg coming through the bedroom ceiling
It's time for me to end this poem, cause you know me I could go on forever
We all love you, miss you and will forget you never
But one more thing I want you to know
This is a warning for you about when it's my time to go

I will bust through the doors of heaven, run and tackle you to the ground
Hug you with the biggest hug to ever give, cause finally my brother I
have found

Abigale's dream is for all health care workers, patients and family members to read this story. Munchausen by Proxy is a relatively uncommon condition that involves the exaggeration or fabrication of illnesses or symptoms by a primary caregiver. It is usually a child, but can be an adult victim and caregiver. An individual deliberately make another person close to them sick, keeps them sick or convinces others that the person is sick. The perpetrator feels satisfied by gaining the attention and sympathy of doctor's, nurses and others who come into contact with him or her and the victim. Some experts believe that it isn't just the attention that's gained from the illness that drives this behavior, but also the satisfaction in being able to deceive individuals that they consider to be more important than themselves. Also monetary gain or not having to work so they can take care of the patient can also be a motive.

Because the caregiver appears to be so caring and attentive, often no one suspects any wrongdoing. A perplexing aspect of this mental illness syndrome is the ability of the caregiver to fool and manipulate doctors. The doctors are usually baffled by what is happening.

Diagnosis of Munchausen by Proxy is very difficult but involves the following clues:

A person who has multiple health problems that don't respond to treatment or that follow a persistent and puzzling coarse
Physical or laboratory findings that are highly unusual, don't correspond with the victim's medical history or physically or clinically impossible
Short-term symptoms that tend to stop when the perpetrator isn't around
A caregiver who isn't reassured by "good news"

A caregiver who's unusually calm in the face of serious difficulties
with the victim's health
A caregiver who appears to be medically knowledgeable or fascinated
with medical details or appears to enjoy the hospital environment
A caregiver who is highly supportive and encouraging of the doctor,
or one who is angry and demands further intervention, more
procedures, second opinions, or transfers to another facility
A victim appears to be afraid to answer or speak without the
permission of the caregiver or appears afraid of the caregiver
Frequent requests of the caregiver for pain medications or other
medications
Caregiver gives false medical or personal history
In some cases, the caregivers were abused, both physically and
sexually as children. They may have come from families in which
being sick was a way to get love
This is a very hard mental health syndrome to prove, and very hard
to catch the perpetrator in the act. They are usually very good at
what they do and very convincing

<u>Munchausen by Proxy cases are resolved in three ways:</u>
The perpetrator is apprehended
The perpetrator moves on to another victim
The victim dies

To help such a person, first of all they must admit to the abuse and
seek psychological treatment. But, if the perpetrator doesn't admit
to any wrongdoing, psychological treatment has little chance of
remedying the situation. Psychotherapy depends on truth and
perpetrators generally live in denial.

Abigale's dream is to help research this mental health syndrome
to bring awareness, even though it is so rare, so no one else will
ever have to go through such an ordeal as Rick did. This was the
Life and Death of a Brave Man. Rick was the strongest man Abigale
ever knew besides Jesus himself. I'm sure Rick is saying "Praise The
Lord". Rick died in the name of Jesus and with God's promises.